Drugs

Series Editor: Cara Acred

Volume 301

Independence Educational Publishers

First published by Independence Educational Publishers

The Studio, High Green

Great Shelford

Cambridge CB22 5EG

England

© Independence 2016

Photocopy licence

The material in this book is protected by copyright. However, the
purchaser is free to make multiple copies of particular articles for instructional
purposes for immediate use within the purchasing institution.
Making copies of the entire book is not permitted.

ISBN-13: 978 1 86168 742 5

Printed in Great Britain
Zenith Print Group

Contents

Introduction

Drugs is Volume 301 in the **ISSUES** series. The aim of the series is to offer current, diverse information about important issues in our world, from a UK perspective.

ABOUT DRUGS

According to statistics, one in 12 adults aged 16 to 59 have taken illicit drugs in the last year. This is equal to 2.8 million people. However, sources claim that trends among young people show a decline in risky behaviours. This book explores the different types and effects of illegal drugs. It also looks at the dangers of legal highs, current statistics and steroid use. The second chapter examines UK drugs laws, and the third chapter goes further still to look at what it really means to have an addiction and how to get help.

OUR SOURCES

Titles in the **ISSUES** series are designed to function as educational resource books, providing a balanced overview of a specific subject.

The information in our books is comprised of facts, articles and opinions from many different sources, including:

⇨ Newspaper reports and opinion pieces

⇨ Website factsheets

⇨ Magazine and journal articles

⇨ Statistics and surveys

⇨ Government reports

⇨ Literature from special interest groups.

A NOTE ON CRITICAL EVALUATION

Because the information reprinted here is from a number of different sources, readers should bear in mind the origin of the text and whether the source is likely to have a particular bias when presenting information (or when conducting their research). It is hoped that, as you read about the many aspects of the issues explored in this book, you will critically evaluate the information presented.

It is important that you decide whether you are being presented with facts or opinions. Does the writer give a biased or unbiased report? If an opinion is being expressed, do you agree with the writer? Is there potential bias to the 'facts' or statistics behind an article?

ASSIGNMENTS

In the back of this book, you will find a selection of assignments designed to help you engage with the articles you have been reading and to explore your own opinions. Some tasks will take longer than others and there is a mixture of design, writing and research-based activities that you can complete alone or in a group.

FURTHER RESEARCH

At the end of each article we have listed its source and a website that you can visit if you would like to conduct your own research. Please remember to critically evaluate any sources that you consult and consider whether the information you are viewing is accurate and unbiased.

Useful weblinks

www.addictionhelper.com

www.addiction-ssa.org

www.aidsmap.com

www.centreforsocialjustice.org.uk

www.theconversation.com

www.drinksmeter.com

www.drugsmeter.com

www.globaldrugsurvey.com

www.gov.uk

www.theguardian.com

www.help4addiction.co.uk

www.heraldscotland.com

www.homeless.org.uk

www.huffingtonpost.co.uk

www.mentoruk.org.uk

www.themixuk.org

www.myrecoverymychoice.co.uk

www.natcen.ac.uk

www.nhs.uk

www.thepharmacist.co.uk

www.telegraph.co.uk

www.unodc.org

young.scot

Get the facts about drugs

What are drugs? Technically speaking, they are chemical substances that affect the normal functioning of the body and/or brain. Not all drugs are illegal. For example, caffeine (found in coffee or Coca-Cola), nicotine (in cigarettes) and alcohol are all technically legal drugs, although they are usually not referred to as such. Medicines, whether prescribed by a doctor or available over the counter at pharmacies, are legal drugs to help us recover from illnesses, although they can also be abused.

Illegal drugs are drugs that are so harmful that countries across the world have decided to control them. Countries have passed several international laws, in the form of United Nations conventions, that specify which drugs are controlled.

All the drugs discussed in this article are illegal. This means that generally, it is against the law to own, use or sell these drugs worldwide.

Drugs tend to have several street names and this article will tell you some of them. However, it is not a complete list and the drugs might have different names in your country or city. These names may also change over time. The street names do not tell you anything about the strength or purity of a drug.

All illegal drugs have immediate physical effects, which you can read about in this article. But drugs can also severely hinder psychological and emotional development, particularly among young people. In fact, drugs can take away potential that users can never get back as drugs substitute the development of other, natural coping mechanisms.

Although each drug is discussed separately in this article, drugs are often used together. This mixing can have unpredictable, severe effects on the body and/or mind of the user.

Drugs cloud the judgement of users. This means that drug users often take more risks, such as having unsafe sex. This can lead to them getting infected with hepatitis or HIV and other sexually transmitted diseases.

There are lots of reasons why people take illegal drugs. Some take them to escape problems while others are bored, curious or just want to feel good. People may be pressured into taking drugs to 'fit in' with a particular crowd or to rebel or get attention.

Drug users come from all kinds of backgrounds. They are male and female, young and old, rich and poor, working and unemployed, from the city and the countryside – it does not matter. Drug use can affect anyone.

While some of the physical effects of drugs might sound nice, they do not last long. Many people get depressed and lonely afterwards and start feeling sick. Also, it is common for people who use drugs to seem confused, have red eyes, sweat a lot and not care about their physical appearance. And, of course, there is the risk of becoming addicted.

Cannabis

Bongo/Ganja/Grass/ Marijuana/Pot/Thai sticks

What is it?

Cannabis is a tobacco-like greenish or brownish material made of the dried flowering tops and leaves of the cannabis (hemp) plant.

Cannabis resin or 'hash' is the dried black or brown secretion of the flowering tops of the cannabis plant, which is made into a powder or pressed into slabs or cakes.

Cannabis oil or 'hash oil' is a liquid extracted from either the dried plant material or the resin.

How is it taken?

All forms of cannabis are usually smoked. Cannabis resin and oil can also be swallowed or brewed in tea.

How does it affect users?

Cannabis can make users feel pleasurably relaxed and sometimes euphoric. Users may also experience a more vivid sense of sight, smell, taste and hearing.

What are the risks associated with cannabis use?

In the short term, users have an increased appetite and pulse rate. Users also have problems performing physical and intellectual tasks such as driving a car and thinking logically.

With large doses, users' perceptions of sound and colour may be sharpened, while their thinking becomes slow and confused. If the dose is very large, the effects of cannabis are similar to those of hallucinogens and may cause anxiety, panic and even psychotic episodes.

Regular users of cannabis risk developing psychological dependence to the point where they lose interest in all other activities, such as work and personal relationships. Recent studies in the United Kingdom show a link between cannabis use and an increase in schizophrenia.

Other risks

Cannabis smoke contains 50 per cent more tar than high-tar cigarettes, which puts users at an increased risk of lung cancer and other respiratory diseases.

Cocaine

Crack/Bazooka/Blanche/ Cake/Coke/Lady

What is it?

Cocaine is a fine white or off-white powder that acts as a powerful stimulant. It is extracted from the leaves of the coca plant. On the street, it can be diluted or 'cut' with other substances to increase the quantity. Crack is cocaine that has been further processed with ammonia or sodium bicarbonate (baking soda) and looks like small flakes or rocks.

How is it taken?

Cocaine is usually sniffed/snorted or injected, whereas crack is smoked.

How does it affect users?

Cocaine can make users feel exhilarated and euphoric. Furthermore, users often experience a temporary increase in alertness and energy levels and delayed hunger and fatigue.

What are the risks associated with cocaine use?

Short-term effects include loss of appetite, faster breathing and increased body temperature and heart rate. Users may behave bizarrely, erratically and sometimes violently.

Excessive doses of cocaine may lead to convulsions, seizures, stroke, cerebral haemorrhage or heart failure.

Long-term users of cocaine risk a number of health problems, some of them depending on how they take the drug. Sniffing cocaine severely damages nose tissue; smoking can cause respiratory problems; whilst injection can lead to abscesses and infectious diseases. Other risks, regardless of how the drug is taken, include strong psychological dependence, malnutrition, weight loss, disorientation, apathy and a state similar to paranoid psychosis.

Other risks

Mixing cocaine with alcohol is a dangerous cocktail and can greatly increase the chances of sudden death.

Ecstasy

E/Snackies/New Yorkers

What is it?

Ecstasy is a psychoactive stimulant, usually made in illegal laboratories. In fact, the term 'ecstasy' has evolved and no longer refers to a single substance but a range of substances similar in effect on users. Frequently, any tablet with a logo is now referred to as 'ecstasy' regardless of its chemical makeup.

While the drug is usually distributed as a tablet, it can also be a powder or capsule. Tablets can have many different shapes and sizes.

How is it taken?

It is usually swallowed but can also be snorted or injected.

How does it affect users?

Ecstasy can heighten users' empathy levels and induce a feeling of closeness to people around them. It can also make users feel more sociable and energetic.

What are the risks associated with ecstasy use?

In the short term, ecstasy can make the body ignore distress signals such as dehydration, dizziness and exhaustion and it can interfere with the body's ability to regulate temperature.

Furthermore, ecstasy can severely damage organs such as the liver and the kidneys. Use can lead to convulsions and heart failure.

Large doses of ecstasy also cause restlessness, anxiety and severe hallucinations.

Long-term ecstasy use can damage certain parts of the brain, resulting in serious depression and memory loss.

Other risks

Tablets or pills that are sold as 'ecstasy' may contain other potentially dangerous substances which can vary widely in strength and effects

Heroin

Smack/H/Horse/Junk/Harry/ White lady

What is it?

Heroin is an addictive drug with pain-killing properties processed from morphine, a naturally occurring substance from the opium poppy plant. Pure heroin is a white powder. Street heroin is usually brownish white because it is diluted or 'cut' with impurities, meaning each dose is different.

How is it taken?

It is usually injected but can also be snorted, smoked or inhaled.

How does it affect users?

Heroin can relieve users' tension, anxiety and depression. Users feel detached from emotional or physical distress or pain. With large doses, users may experience euphoria.

What are the risks associated with heroin use?

Short-term effects include constricted pupils, nausea, vomiting, drowsiness, inability to concentrate and apathy.

Heroin is very addictive and users may quickly develop physical and psychological dependence. They also risk developing tolerance for the drug, which means they need constantly higher doses to achieve the effect they want.

Long-term heroin use has a variety of severe health effects.

Among other things, it can cause severe weight loss, malnutrition and constipation. It can also lead to menstrual irregularity, sedation and chronic apathy.

Abruptly quitting heroin use leads to withdrawal symptoms which can be severe such as cramps, diarrhoea, tremors, panic, runny nose, chills and sweats.

Other risks

Users risk overdosing on heroin, which can lead to coma and death through respiratory depression.

LSD

Acid/Hippie
What is it?

LSD is a semi-synthetic drug derived from lysergic acid, which is found in a fungus that grows on rye and other grains.

LSD, commonly referred to as "acid", is usually sold on the street as small squares of blotting paper with drops containing the drug. It can also be sold as tablets, capsules or occasionally in liquid form. It is a colourless, odourless substance with a slightly bitter taste.

How is it taken?

It is usually swallowed.

How does it affect users?

Taking LSD leads to strong changes in thought, mood and senses in addition to feelings of empathy and sociability. However, the exact effects of LSD vary depending on the mental state of the user and the environment when taking the drug.

What are the risks associated with LSD use?

Short term, LSD produces delusions and distorted perceptions. The user's sense of depth and time changes and colours, sound and touch seem more intense.

Some LSD users experience severe, terrifying thoughts and feelings such as fear of losing control, fear of insanity and death, and despair.

The physical effects are small compared to the psychological and emotional effects. They include dilated pupils, increased heart rate and blood pressure, loss of appetite, sleeplessness, dry mouth and tremors.

Methamphetamine

Crack meth/Ice/Crystal meth/Tik/Shabu/Yaba
What is it?

Methamphetamine is part of the group of drugs called amphetamine-type stimulants (ATS). It is a synthetic drug that is usually manufactured in illegal laboratories.

Methamphetamine comes as a powder, tablet or as crystals that look like shards of glass.

How is it taken?

It can be swallowed, sniffed/snorted, smoked or injected.

How does it affect users?

Methamphetamine stimulates a feeling of physical and mental well being, as well as a surge of euphoria and exhilaration. Users experience a temporary rise in energy, often perceived to improve their performance at manual or intellectual tasks. Users also experience delayed hunger and fatigue.

> **"Heroin is very addictive and users may quickly develop physical and psychological dependence"**

What are the risks associated with methamphetamine use?

Short term, users can lose their appetite and start breathing faster. Their heart rate and blood pressure may increase and their body temperature may rise and cause sweating. With large doses, users can feel restless and irritable and can experience panic attacks.

Excessive doses of methamphetamine can lead to convulsions, seizures and death from respiratory failure, stroke or heart failure.

Long term methamphetamine use can lead to malnutrition, weight loss and the development of psychological dependence.

Once chronic users stop taking methamphetamine, a long period of sleep, and then depression, usually follows.

Other risks

Methamphetamine use sometimes triggers aggressive, violent and bizarre behaviour among users.

⇨ The above information is reprinted with kind permission from the United Nations Office on Drugs and Crime (UNODC). Please visit www.unodc.org for further information.

Smoking, drinking and drug use: new trends and what they mean

By Michael O'Toole

The latest instalment of the Health and Social Care Information Centre's (HSCIC) ongoing survey of young people[1], published on 23 July 2015, sheds light on several issues that continue to whirl around media and public opinion.

Since the 1980s, the *Smoking, Drinking and Drug Use Among Young People in England* series has been a valuable indicator of current and emerging trends in young people's attitudes towards drug use. This year's report confirms the continuation of a number of positive trends, highlights areas for improvement, and, for the first time, provides useful insight into the scale of the NPS problem among young people.

Broad trends are overwhelmingly positive

The number of 11- to 15-year-olds who have tried alcohol is at its lowest level (38%) since the survey began, and only 8% drank in the last week. There are a number of potential reasons for this ongoing decline – DEMOS recently reported[2] that social media is cited as a distraction and/or a deterrent to heavy drinking for as many as four in ten young people – but it appears that the trend is due to a mix of changing attitudes towards health and drunkenness, as well as the impact of migrants from non-drinking cultures.

But the numbers should still be treated with caution: HSCIC estimates suggest that 240,000 11-to-15-year-olds drank in the last week, representing a significant amount of underage drinking; and almost one in ten young people drank 15 units or more. Further, these cases of heavy underage drinking are linked to other risky behaviours, including smoking, drug use and truancy, suggesting that there is a need to target prevention initiatives at a significant minority of vulnerable young people.

The role of parents

The survey also highlighted the profound influence of parents on young people's drinking behaviour. Only 2% of pupils who said their parents did not like them to drink had drunk alcohol in the last week, compared to 44% of those whose parents did not mind. Along with the fact that families are one of the main sources of procuring alcohol, this strengthens the evidence that parents can be one of the most important protective factors in young peoples' lives.

HSCIC findings with regard to other drugs were similarly positive: the number of 11- to 15-year-olds who have ever smoked (19%) is as low as it has ever been and, although the decline has slowed, fewer school-aged children have ever taken illegal drugs.

Given the tone of media reporting[3] – headlines such as, "Will your child die from a legal high?" and "Primary school kids taking legal highs" – data on NPS is particularly intriguing. 2.5% of young people had tried an New Psychoactive Substances (NPS), compared to 15% who had taken illicit drugs, most commonly cannabis; and despite being the 'legal high capital of Europe', only half of respondents had heard of 'legal highs'.

The role of schools

Finally, the survey elicited insight into the status of drug education in schools. Echoing Mentor's findings in 2013[4], HSCIC report that the vast majority of schools provide one lesson per year on smoking, drinking and drug use, with fewer than one in ten schools offering lessons more than once a term. Consequently, satisfaction with drug education has decreased in recent years: today, 60% of young people think schools gave enough information about smoking, 56% about drinking and 54% about drug use; and almost half of young people could not recall learning about any of these.

Therefore, despite a continual downward trend in drug use and some improvements in drug education, including the ongoing development of Mentor-ADEPIS (mentor-adepis.org), there are still some areas of concern. In particular, there is a need to target the most vulnerable young people, who are often susceptible to a range of interlinked risky behaviours. The report also highlights certain widely reported problems that are perhaps not as serious as popular opinion suggests. Although NPS remain a concern, their use is not prevalent among 11- to 15-year-olds, which suggests that a holistic approach to drug education and prevention at an early age remains the best way to protect young people from a range of interconnected risks.

29 July 2015

⇨ The above information is reprinted with kind permission from Mentor UK. Please visit www.mentoruk.org.uk for further information.

1 *Smoking, Drinking and Drug Use Among Young People in England – 2014 [NS].* Health & Social Care Information Centre. Published July 23, 2015. Accessed March 14 2016. http://www.hscic.gov.uk/catalogue/PUB17879.

2 Owen, Jonathan. 2015. *Forget Pubs And Clubs, Today's Youth Would Rather Be On Social Media.* The Independent. Accessed March 14 2016. http://www.independent.co.uk/life-style/gadgets-and-tech/news/temptations-of-alcohol-being-replaced-by-lure-of-social-media-for-many-young-britons-says-new-study-10391081.html.

3 *Kids These Days Are Smoking And Drinking A Lot Less Than They Used To.* 2016. The Huffington Post UK. Accessed March 14 2016. http://www.huffingtonpost.co.uk/2015/07/23/children-drug-use-alcohol-smoking-legal-highs-kill_n_7855548.html.

4 *"We Don't Get Taught Enough": An Assessment Of Drug Education Provision In Schools In England: Drugs And Alcohol Today: Vol 15, No 3.* 2016. Drugs And Alcohol Today. http://www.emeraldinsight.com/doi/abs/10.1108/DAT-03-2015-0014.

Statistical news release – drug misuse: findings from the 2014/15 crime survey

Survey for England and Wales.

The latest National Statistics on illicit drug use in England and Wales are released today, based on self-reported data from the 2014/15 Crime Survey for England and Wales (CSEW).

Key findings:

⇨ Around one in 12 (8.6%) adults aged 16 to 59 had taken an illicit drug in the last year. This equated to around 2.8 million people. This was similar to the 2013/14 survey estimate (8.8%, 2.9 million).

⇨ According to the 2014/15 CSEW, 3.2% of adults aged 16 to 59 had taken a Class A drug in the last year, equivalent to just over one million people. The long-term trend in Class A drug use has been broadly stable over the last few years, although there has been some fluctuation.

⇨ Use of New Psychoactive Substances (NPS) in the last year appears to be concentrated among young adults aged 16 to 24. Around one in 40 (2.8%) young adults aged 16 to 24 took an NPS in the last year, while fewer than one in 100 (0.9%) of 16- to 59-year-olds had done so. This equates to around 174,000 young adults aged 16 to 24 and 279,000 adults aged 16 to 59.

⇨ The use of ecstasy in the last year increased among 16- to 24-year-olds between the 2013/14 and 2014/15 surveys, from 3.9% to 5.4%. This is an increase of approximately 95,000 young people.

Other findings from the 2014/15 CSEW

Frequency of illicit drug use in the last year

⇨ Estimates from the 2014/15 CSEW show that 2.2% of adults aged 16 to 59 were classed as frequent drug users (having taken any illicit drug more than once a month on average in the last year). Frequent drug users made up just over a third (36%) of the adults who reported drug use within the last year. The 2014/15 CSEW showed that 8% of adults who reported using drugs last year said they had used drugs every day.

⇨ Cannabis was the drug most likely to be frequently used, with 39% of cannabis users being classed as frequent users in the 2014/15 survey. Tranquillisers were the second most likely drug type to be used (27% of users reported frequent use in the 2013/14 survey – the most recent data available on frequency of using drugs other than cannabis).

Illicit drug use by personal, household and area characteristics and lifestyle factors

⇨ Younger people are more likely to take drugs than older people. The level of any drug use in the last year was highest among 16- to 19-year-olds (18.8%) and 20- to 24-year-olds (19.8%). The level of drug use was much lower in the oldest age group surveyed (2.4% of 55- to 59-year-olds).

⇨ People living in urban areas reported higher levels of drug use than those living in rural areas. Just under a tenth (9.1%) of people living in urban areas had used any drug compared with 6.5% of those living in rural areas. In addition, higher levels of drug use are associated with increased frequency of visits to pubs, bars and nightclubs.

Simultaneous polydrug and polysubstance use

⇨ In the combined 2013/14 and 2014/15 surveys, 9% of respondents who used drugs in the last year said that the last time they used drugs, they used more than one drug at the same time. This has increased significantly from 7% in the combined 2010/11 and 2011/12 surveys.

⇨ Mephedrone (68%), ecstasy (57%), amphetamines (50%) and tranquillisers (35%) were the drugs most likely to be used simultaneously with other drugs. The lowest prevalence of polydrug use was found among those who had used cannabis the last time they had used drugs (9% of those who used cannabis last time used it alongside another drug).

23 July 2015

⇨ The above information is reprinted with kind permission from the Home Office. Please visit www.gov.uk for further information.

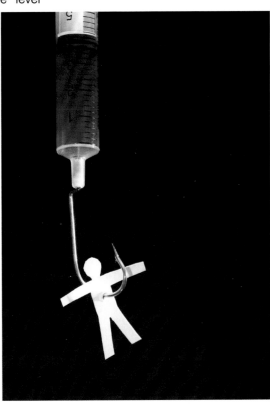

The Global Drug Survey 2015 findings

An overview of our key findings.

Dr Adam R Winstock, Founder Director GDS

Well, first, just how generous were people with their time?

We estimate that over the duration of the study (Nov–Dec 2014) over 100,000 people spent in excess of:

⇨ four million minutes, or

⇨ 67,000 hours, or

⇨ 2,800 days, or

⇨ 400 weeks, or

⇨ 7.5 years sharing their drug use experiences with us.

So a HUGE thanks to you all. GDS does not exist without you.

I also want to acknowledge the unbelievable help that all our partners and the academic network and harm reduction groups around the world provide with revising and translating the survey then working so closely with all our media partners. In particular, I want to acknowledge the vital role that Dr Jason Ferris, our chief biostats man, has provided with the analysis and production of reports. Thanks mate.

Well, working our way from the more common to less commonly used drugs these are some of interesting things we found out

Alcohol

Ireland's reputation for heavy drinking is well deserved. Not only did Ireland have higher rates of drinkers at risk of dependence (AUDIT score of 20 or more), they report needing to drink more alcohol than almost any other country to get as drunk as they would want to be but they also had the highest rates of getting more drunk more often than they wanted to, thinking their doctor would tell them to drink less, attending A&E after drinking more often and perhaps thankfully the highest proportion of drinkers who want to drink less in the coming year.

But the Irish stereotype aside (Australia, The Netherlands, UK and NZ you can't smile) I was struck by two things.

There is NOT a fine line between getting as drunk as you would want get and being more drunk than you want. It's about a 30% line. Now, not only is the mean amount of alcohol about 90gm for women and 120gm for men – about five times above what the WHO advise as the maximum amount to drink in a day.

So with 20-25% of people on average saying they were getting more drunk more often than they wanted to ('tippled' at least monthly) here is my advice. When you get to the place you feel as intoxicated with alcohol as you want to, SLOW your drinking down. The tipping point for many people is just one or two drinks, so if you want to have a better, cheaper healthier night, just slow down and drink a little less. Want some advice, go to www.drinksmeter.com or get it free on the app stores.

The other thing I learned is how different things motivate different groups to change their drinking, with social embarrassment being a huge motivator for many, especially the Germans, Swiss, Austrians and the Aussies. If you want to see how much of an ARSE (stands for Alcohol Related Social Embarrassment score) you are when you drink try the GSS One Too Many test at www.onetoomany.co.

Tobacco

For tobacco we learned that far to many cannabis smokers continue to mix their weed/resin with tobacco and that we should strive to be like Americans or the Kiwis. And for all the fears over e-cigarettes while many smokers have tried them the proportion who go on to become daily users is very small, though last year prevalence in many countries is increasing. More

e-ciggie companies for the tobacco companies to buy I guess.

Cannabis

And while high-potency herbal cannabis dominates the world market and carries the greatest risk of harms it seems other types can also land you in the emergency department as well.

Sadly the uptake of vapourisers by the cannabis – using community is still in its infancy – lots of lungs to be saved from harm out there.

While high-potency cannabis remains dominant we learned that butane hash oil (BHO) is starting to nudge its way into the cannabis–using community with over 2,500 people sharing their thoughts on this new form of cannabis. Faster, stronger and possibly with higher risks of swifter development of tolerance and withdrawal it's too early to pass judgement. It does allow for other methods of use to be adopted however, as shown below, and this might be a good thing.

Hopefully more balanced BHO oils will appear and will encourage the use of vape pens so the typical trajectory of increased potency leading to increased problematic use and dependence can be exchanged for greater control and harm reduction. For this to be a reality the marijuana industry needs to get on board and provide an index to inform customers of risks and how to avoid them. And given one in four reported making BHO at home, some occupational health and safety advice on choice of solvent, the need for good ventilation and to avoid unsightly explosions are probably needed. GDS will launch the world's first ever safer drug use limits – starting with the cannabis guidelines on 17 June.

Synthetic cannabis

But while BHO may be the new 'natural kid on the block', GDS's work on synthetic cannabinoids continues to cause great concern. For the third year running these drugs were more to likely to leave people needing emergency medical treatment than any other group we explored this year – with 3.5% of last year users reporting having sought EMT in the last year a (30% increase from 2.5% last year). The risk increased to one in eight users who reported using 100 or more times. This confirms our work published in March that the risk of seeking EMT was 30 times higher with SC products than high-potency herbal cannabis (skunk, hydro). Our findings also highlighted the risk of dependence on these drugs with over 60% of those using 50 or more times reporting withdrawal symptoms on cessation. While herbal preparations remain the most common we also saw the appearance of crystal, resin and liquid forms.

Why?

GDS remains confused as to why there remains a market for such an unsafe and less pleasant drug than the natural alternative. Our findings on the motivations among users of novel psychoactive substances (NPS) however, suggests that price might be a key driver, with the average gram of synthetic cannabis (SC) costing €8 vs. €12 for weed, with most people getting ten joints from a gram of SC vs. three from a gram of natural. Among some groups where access to natural cannabis is difficult there may be a greater attraction – such as prisons (where I work part time) and where people wish to avoid detection in drug screens. Think your train drivers, miners and truckers! Profits margins are huge, export is easy and regulation unenforceable. Perhaps cannabis dealers might like to lower the price of their produce, offer something other than high THC weed and governments consider if their regulation efforts on cannabis like products might be focused elsewhere? Maybe even offer some safe using limit guidelines for cannabis now it's legal in some places. Oh hang on GDS is already doing that and releasing them in mid June!

Other novel psychoactive drugs (NPS)

Synthetic cannabinoids whilst the most numerous in terms of new notifications and market share are not the only class of NPS being marketed and used out there. And while GDS wont jump in the media scare mongering we did find that the rate seeking EMT on NPS generally was at least three times greater than for traditional illicit drugs.

Unknown potency, limited honest product information (due to government regulation) and varied effect and risk profiles make shiny packets not a great way to get high. But, as usual, the factors leading to people seeking EMT on new drugs are pretty similar to the risks with old. The GDS poem for new drug takers is "If you take a drug you do not know our advice start low go slow and ask a mate to keep an eye on you cos you never know with something new". If governments are going to "ban all new drugs that get you high" then they need to better educate people who use traditional drugs to use them more safely. The GDS *High-Way Code* does exactly this.

Research chemicals – trends in use

They're on the decline. They may be more numerous but GDS has spotted a year decline in the UK and this has been noted elsewhere. Why? Because beyond being cheap, most of these new drugs offer less desirable and a more risky experience than the traditional drugs used across the world. And given drug use is a goal-orientated behaviour with consumers making generally smart informed decisions around what they use, unless new drugs convey significant advantage in one or more domains (and price for some is very important) few will catch on.

The UK still uses more than most but really with the re-emergence of better quality traditional drugs and the dark net I am unsure where these much hyped drugs are going in most countries.

Cocaine

Cocaine remains the most expensive drug per gram in the world (cannabis seeds are the most expensive though not strictly a drug of course). Most users (80%) use less than ten times in the last 12 months in most countries at a mean price of €70, the average of consumed dose of 1/2gm seems to be an example of harm reduction by price (minimum pricing in the UK). NZ and Australia remain the priciest place to buy cocaine in the world – why – because their border control is great and the size of the markets they offer to cartels is small. The presence of crystal meth also helps (or not, since it is a drug with whole loads more problems for users in most cases). Certainly, cocaine markets have responded to the possibility of competition and low satisfaction with their product with a global two-tier market both at ounce/kilo level and street dealing gram levels. And before you think of going to Brazil for cocaine don't, but you have to wait till they come out with their findings later this month to find out why.

Potency and problems

But the Emergency Room and the Accident & Emergency Dept are not only the preserve of those taking new drugs, and clearly on a population level and when considering the public health and economic costs, alcohol wins hands down. No surprise there but we were kind of shocked that 1% of last year cannabis users had sought EMT in the previous 12 months (compared to 1.2% of drinkers). That's a lot of people who are using a drug that we kind of think of as not that risky at least in the short term. Now while most reported feeling 'back to normal' within a day, overwhelmingly they'd smoked high potency weed – so once again potency ain't always a good thing. Again, we hope some guidelines might help.

MDMA – sometimes bigger is not better

Now I know some people will give me a hard time if I keep on about the emergency room and acute drug problems, but we also saw a tripling in the number of last year MDMA users seeking EMT from 0.3% in GDS2013 to 0.6% in GDS2014 to 0.9 in GDS2015. Now although it's important to note that GDS2013 was predominately UK, AU and USA whilst GDS2014 and GDS2015 involved much larger samples and more countries, the trend is striking and worries me that better quality MDMA in pill or powder form, taken unwisely places people at greater risk of harm.

Don't be making pills with 200mg + of MDMA in them please

Now although we saw a huge increase in participation rates and countries over those years you can escape the fact pills and MDMA crystal are about in abundance. Sometimes these pills contain in excess of 200mg and occasionally 300mg of MDMA, twice and three times what most people think is a reasonable dose. While the mean amount of MDMA consumed over a session seems to be about 1/4gm some countries are going way above that. No surprise that it is the UK topping the list at a whacking mean dose of 0.42mg/session. I asked *Vice*'s Dutch editor Thijs Roes who had interviewed several pill producers what he thought was behind the production of these super dose pills. He told me: "What they're doing is basically a pissing contest. One told me it was a competition between manufacturers and a race against themselves. The other described his 330mg pill as a flagship product, as a way to get known in the scene. They felt that users would know to dose them, and that the amount of MDMA would eventually stabilise around 200mg." Our request would be make standard pills of 80–100mg and put the dosage on them – way more useful than logos for all concerned, and if you are knocking out 200mg pills put a big groove down the middle so people figure out they should just take half (or even better a quarter). Every time you get a new pill always take a quarter to start with and wait at least 60–90 minutes before dosing: "start low go slow".

All of this combined with frequent consumption with alcohol and combining pills and powder explains the high rates of EMT we are seeing.

What it says to me is that better quality drugs can cause more harm that rubbish ones – unless you know what your taking. Once again so many of these admissions could have been avoided with some common sense – see the GDS *High-Way Code* for a safer use guide voted for by 80,000 people.

Nitrous oxide/laughing gas

Some drugs sit in that grey area of legal versus not. Nitrous oxide is such a drug. And it remains true that a few balloons taken every now and then, somewhere safe and when you're not already 'munted' is not going to do you any harm but our data from almost 7,000 last year users offers some words of caution. First thing is the big increase between GDS2014 and GDS2015 is people who reported being worried about the impact of nitrous oxide on their physical health – tripling from 2.5% to over 7.5%. Second is that nitrous oxide inactivates Vitamin B12. Lack of that vitamin – commonly in vegetarians can cause anaemia and nerve damage – called a peripheral neuropathy. Our findings last year suggested a strong dose response relationship between the amount you used in a session and frequency of use people reporting numbness and tingling persisting after use – a sign of peripheral neuropathy. This year with smarter questions developed with the help of a neurologist (thanks to Dr Paul Hart) our data seems to indicate even more clearly that somewhere in the region of 4% of last year users are reporting symptoms consistent with a peripheral neuropathy (numbness/tingling in face, arms, mouth, legs/shooting pains in limbs that persisted for weeks after last use). There was strong relationship with how much and how often people used. So if you use balloons, notice persistent numbness/tingling in your fingers/toes or around your mouth/face or notice you are off balance or are finding it hard to operate your phone – go see your doctor. Investigated and managed quickly the condition should be reversible. This is no laughing matter (the pun is intentional) and while we fear the media will come up with a headline like "hippy crack causes paralysis" (thanks to Dr Stephen Kaar

for that), we do just want to let people know that if you use a lot there are risks. You can avoid those risks by not using too much too often. I don't think we need to regulate just educate... Our safer use advice is given below.

Don't inhale directly from the charger

⇨ Avoid mixing in nitrous when you are off your face on other drugs, especially alcohol

⇨ Try not to use more than five balloons in a session and leave time between them

⇨ Make sure any space you are using is well ventilated

⇨ Don't use near roads, canals or other bodies of water

⇨ Make sure you got mates around you in case you fall over and hurt yourself

⇨ Leave several minutes between rounds of hits and give yourself breaks between periods of use to refill those vitamin stores. Animal protein (beef and fish in particular), eggs, cheese are good sources of B12. Fortified soy products and supplements can be used by vegetarians. And Marmite!!!

⇨ If you experience persistent numbness, tingling or weakness in your fingers, hands or feet, or notice you're having difficulty typing or losing your balance or coordination strop using and go see your doctor

⇨ Finally there are reports that cheap whipped cream bulbs imported for China leave an oily residue when the gas evaporates – probably making them unfit to dispense cream let alone to inhale. So if you are going to inhale try accessing your gas from a quality supplier.

⇨ The above information is from the Global Drug Survey. Visit www.globaldrugsurvey.com for more information.

⇨ For anonymous, personalised feedback about your drinking or drug use visit www.drinksmeter.com or www.drugsmeter.com.

© Global Drug Survey 2016

A legal substance does not equal to a safe substance

Carole Fox of Sifa Fireside looks at this issue, which is having an increasing impact on homelessness services and the people they support.

As an agency experienced in supporting people with complex needs as a result of alcohol, substance misuse and mental health issues, our team have the skills to address certain types of behaviour. However, around two years ago we began to notice a distinct change in the behaviour of the people accessing our service.

From chatting with clients it started to emerge that this pronounced change was down to the use of 'legal highs'. This became even more of an issue when those who had traditionally used Class A substances and/or alcohol began to combine legal and illegal substances.

What are 'legal highs'?

These substances combine a range of chemicals that produce effects similar to illegal drugs like ecstasy, cocaine and marijuana. They are often marketed as plant food or bath salts, and the wide range of ingredients used means it is almost impossible for users to know exactly what they are taking and the damage it may cause.

What are the effects?

The physical reaction to these substances is often dramatic. When a client has used legal highs there is a possibility that they will 'drop like a stone' to the floor and their complexion will take on a green and yellowish tone. On occasion they have also appeared extremely psychotic, and we've even had one incident in which a client stopped breathing and staff had to administer first aid to resuscitate him whilst waiting for the ambulance.

Why so popular?

The current appeal of legal highs is primarily based on cost, ease of accessibility and, perhaps most importantly, legality. These products are extremely cheap and can be bought over the counter on the high street from 'head shops', no questions asked.

This means that users don't have to rely on dealers and the risks that go along with this, and there is nothing the police can do if they are found to have a legal high substance on them.

One of the biggest dangers is in users interpreting a 'legal' substance as being a 'safe' substance, which we know is far from the truth. There is also often a misconception that these products are not very strong, so users consume large amounts to achieve the desired effect. They are often cut with chemicals that are not safe for human consumption and, worryingly, are more likely to be used for other purposes, like industrial cleaning.

What can homelessness agencies do?

Our drop-in service was becoming increasingly difficult to manage as a result, so I decided that I needed to know more and attended a training course to gain better insight and awareness of the issue. Following this, our alcohol recovery worker and training manager devised a briefing that could be rolled out to staff, clients and volunteers.

We now offer a specialist training session which gives an overview of the legal highs market, the potential effect on users and practical advice on working with these clients.

What should be done to tackle this issue?

I believe much more awareness and information of the effects and impact of legal highs is needed. I would like to see more done to outlaw these substances, but until then we need greater education and specialist advice.

Despite how it is often perceived, this is not simply a 'night clubbing' issue. In many cases, the ease of access to legal highs is legitimising the destructive behaviours and patterns of abuse that have led people into homelessness, and blocking their journey to recovery.

For example, one client advised me that he is on licence and whilst he would be in serious trouble of going back to prison if he was in possession of illegal substances, there is nothing the police can do about him consuming legal highs. This client has been hospitalised twice in the last six weeks.

As a support agency we have delivered awareness sessions for clients and advised them clearly that legal highs cannot be consumed on our premises. We have also warned clients about sharing cigarettes as there have been several incidences of people unwittingly smoking a legal high.

We have had to deal with people collapsing, call an ambulance for a client who became psychotic and perform CPR on another who collapsed in the drop-in and stopped breathing. These individuals were the lucky ones, because we were able to help. But if the use of legal highs continues to grow in popularity, deaths as a result of their use may become increasingly common.

17 November 2014

⇨ The above information is reprinted with kind permission from Homeless Link. Please visit www.homeless.org.uk for further information.

What is... over-the-counter medicine misuse?

By Niamh Fingleton

Over-the-counter (OTC) medicines are medicines which can be obtained and supplied without a prescription. They are also known as non-prescription medicines. Examples of OTC medicines include analgesics (e.g. paracetamol, ibuprofen and certain codeine-containing analgesics), cold and flu products (e.g. Night Nurse), sleep aids (e.g. Nytol and Sominex), etc. Whilst OTC medicines are often perceived by the public as being safer than prescription medicines, they have the potential to cause harm. All OTC medicines have the potential to be used incorrectly, whilst some have the potential to cause dependence. Cooper (2013a) identified three main categories of harm in his literature review of OTC medicine abuse:

⇨ Direct harms related to the pharmacological or psychological effects of the drug, e.g. dependence to codeine.

⇨ Physiological harms related to the adverse effects of another active ingredient in a compound formulation, e.g. adverse effects of ibuprofen in compound analgesics containing ibuprofen and codeine.

⇨ Harms related to other consequences such as progression to abuse of other substances, economic costs and effects on personal and social life.

OTC medicines most frequently associated with dependence are those capable of causing physical symptoms such tolerance and withdrawal i.e. codeine-containing analgesics and smoking cessation products containing nicotine (Cooper 2013b, Nielsen, Cameron and Pahoki 2010, Hughes et al. 2004). However, the psychological aspects of dependence may occur with any.

The evidence regarding dependence on OTC medicines is sparse. A research team at the University of Aberdeen recently conducted a postal survey of the UK general population (n=946) to determine the prevalence of OTC medicine dependence. A response rate of 43.4% was achieved. The lifetime prevalence was 2%; 0.8% were currently dependent whilst 1.3% had been dependent in the past (Fingleton et al. 2014). When asked what they were dependent on, codeine-containing analgesics were the most frequently mentioned (n=4), e.g. Syndol and Solpadeine. Other OTC medicines mentioned were analgesics without codeine, a sleep aid and a smoking cessation product. Of the eight individuals ever dependent on an OTC medicine, five had never sought help, two sought help from a GP and one had sought help from family and friends. A recent survey of community pharmacies asked about products they perceived to be misused. Codeine-containing products were most frequently suspected of misuse (Matheson, Bond and Robertson 2014).

Previous qualitative research conducted in the UK with people dependent on OTC medicines found there was considerable variation in the perceived benefit of various treatment and support options used by participants; attempts at self-treatment were often ineffective and experiences with general practitioners varied considerably (Cooper 2013b). Specialist treatment services were perceived as not being set-up to treat OTC medicine dependence.

Further research is currently being conducted by the research team at the University of Aberdeen as part of a PhD project funded by the SSA. A qualitative study is currently underway with people who have ever been dependent on OTC medicines to identify the barriers and enablers to seeking treatment, and a survey of specialist drug misuse treatment providers will be conducted in the near future to see how OTC medicine dependence is managed in these settings.

References

Cooper, R. (2013a) *Over-the-counter medicine abuse - a review of the literature*, Journal of Substance Use, 18(2), pp. 82-107.

Cooper, R.J. (2013b) *'I can't be an addict. I am.' Over-the-counter medicine abuse: a qualitative study*, BMJ Open, 3(6), pp. 1-9.

Fingleton, N., Matheson, C., Watson, M. and Duncan, E. (2014) *Non-prescription medicine misuse and dependence in the UK: a general population survey*, Health Services Research and Pharmacy Practice. Aberdeen, April 3-4.

Hughes, J.R., Pillitteri, J.L., Callas, P.W., Callahan, R. and Kenny, M. (2004) *Misuse of and dependence on over-the-counter nicotine gum in a volunteer sample*, Nicotine & Tobacco Research, 6(1), pp. 79-84.

Matheson, C., Bond, C.and Robertson, H. (2014) Community Pharmacy Services for Drug misusers: *Measuring National Service Delivery and the Development of professional Attitudes and Practice over two decades. Report to Chief Scientist Office, Scottish Government.* (Report awaiting approval).

Nielsen, S., Cameron, J. and Pahoki, S. (2010) Final report 2010: *Over the counter codeine dependence*, Victoria: Turning Point Alcohol and Drug Centre.

February 2015

⇨ Information from the Society for the Study of Addiction. www.addiction-ssa.org.

Drugs and the brain

Martin Barnes of DrugScope and neuroscientist Professor David Nutt explain the results of research into the effects of recreational drugs on the brain.

Acid (LSD) and magic mushrooms

Short term: Acid and magic mushrooms are hallucinogenic, making people see, hear and experience the world in a different, 'trippy' way. Colours may become intensified and sounds distorted. Users may also become panicky and suffer from paranoia. The effects of acid can last 12 hours or more which, if it's a bad trip, can be very frightening.

Long term: Some LSD users experience flashbacks. "Sometimes people may experience psychosis or paranoia, believing or seeing things that aren't really there," says Barnes.

Cannabis (marijuana, weed, dope, skunk)

Short term: People smoke cannabis to relax and get high, but it can make it difficult to remember things, even if they've only just happened. It can cause anxiety attacks or feelings of paranoia. "If you use a lot of cannabis regularly, you're putting yourself at risk of some temporary problems, such as confusion or delusions," says Barnes.

Long term: "It's possible that cannabis might trigger long-term mental health problems, including psychosis, schizophrenia and depression," says Barnes. "Evidence suggests that cannabis users who come from a family with a history of mental health problems may be particularly susceptible to these symptoms."

Cocaine and crack cocaine

Short term: Cocaine is a stimulant that makes you feel high, confident and full of energy. But this can turn into feelings of anxiety, panic and paranoia. Users of cocaine can end up feeling tired and depressed.

Long term: Giving up cocaine and crack can be mentally distressing and physically difficult for dependent users. Long-term use can worsen existing mental health problems and lead to depression, anxiety and paranoia.

Ecstasy (E)

Short term: Ecstasy is a stimulant with hallucinogenic effects that makes you feel relaxed, high, 'loved-up' and ready to dance all night. But people who are already feeling anxious or who take high doses can have bad experiences of paranoia or feeling 'out of it'.

Long term: Regular use may lead to sleep problems, lack of energy, drastic weight loss, depression or anxiety. People can become psychologically dependent on the feelings of euphoria and calmness that ecstasy gives them. Research shows that taking ecstasy can reduce a user's serotonin levels, and may have an effect on certain areas of the brain.

Heroin (smack, diamorphine)

Short term: Heroin and other opiates slow down the body's functions and stop both physical and emotional pain. Users find they need to take more and more herion to get the same effect, or even feel 'normal'. Taking a lot can lead to coma or even death.

Long term: Heroin is psychologically and physically highly addictive. "The withdrawal from heroin is really unpleasant," says Professor Nutt. "Long-term heroin users are often depressed because of their overall lifestyle." Coming off and staying off heroin can be very difficult.

Ketamine (K)

Short term: Ketamine is an anaesthetic that makes people feel relaxed and high, but its effects are unpredictable. "It's like drinking a whole bottle of vodka: you don't have any control over what you're doing," says Professor Nutt.

"The biggest danger is wandering off in a daze and having an accident or getting lost and staying out all night, resulting in hypothermia." Ketamine can make you feel detached from yourself and others, and make existing mental health problems worse.

Long term: Tolerance develops quickly so people need more K to get high. "The longer term effects are more difficult to pinpoint, but may include flashbacks and losing your memory and ability to concentrate," says Barnes. "Occasionally, people get psychotic symptoms, while evidence is growing that long-term use of ketamine can severely damage the bladder. Some people find it hard to stop taking K."

Solvents (gases, glues and aerosols)

Short term: Solvents make you feel drunk and sometimes cause hallucinations.

Long term: Heavy use of solvents poisons your brain and can damage it, making it hard to control your emotions, think straight or remember things.

Speed and crystal meth (amphetamine and methamphetamine)

Short term: Speed can quickly make you feel energetic and confident

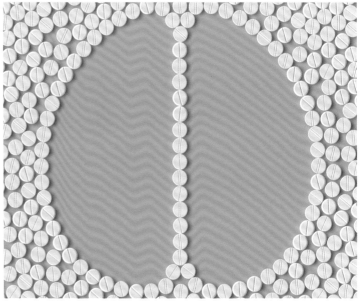

but, with the high, can come panic, irritability and a paranoid sense that everyone is looking at you. Smoking a version of speed called methamphetamine (crystal meth) can give an intense and prolonged high but a severe comedown, when feelings of hopelessness and sadness are common.

Long term: There's no research on the long-term heavy use of speed. Professor Nutt has seen users, especially those who have injected speed regularly, who appear to be permanently depressed. They have difficulty thinking straight, remembering things, problem solving and coping with their emotions.

Steroids

Short term: Steroids pump up muscle mass but can bring on 'roid rage', with users becoming physically violent and sexually abusive. Steroids can make sleep difficult and cause confusion, depression and paranoia.

Long term: They can lead to psychological dependence, where people become convinced they cannot perform well without the drug.

Tranquillisers (benzodiazepines)

Short term: Tranquillisers such as Valium are sedative drugs. They are used to relieve anxiety and aid sleep. Some drug users take them to help a comedown from drugs such as cocaine or speed.

Long term: The body quickly gets used to benzodiazepines and soon needs more to get the same effect. It's possible to become addicted in just a few weeks and withdrawal can be difficult and make people feel sick, unable to sleep and very anxious. Sudden withdrawal from high doses can be very dangerous and result in serious convulsions (fits).

9 October 2014

⇨ The above information is reprinted with kind permission from NHS Choices. Please visit www.nhs.uk for further information.

Thousands of children kicked out of school for drink and drugs, says Centre for Social Justice

There are more than 7,000 exclusions in schools in England each year for drugs or alcohol, the Centre for Social Justice (CSJ) has said.

The damning new statistics, revealed by CSJ analysis of new government data, show how alcohol and drug abuse are daily realities in some of England's state schools.

Christian Guy, former Director of the CSJ, said: "These new figures show many schools are struggling to cope and pupils are being hit by drugs and alcohol and an early age."

Many individual local authorities had several hundreds of pupils excluded for drugs and alcohol – with the highest number in Kent, where there were 272 exclusions.

In total there were 7,400 drug- and alcohol-related exclusions in England, 360 of them permanent.

The CSJ is urging the Government to scrap the drugs information website, FRANK and develop an effective replacement programme to send a strong signal to young people about the dangers of drug and alcohol abuse.

The figures also show that there were 2,550 exclusions from school for sexual misconduct, while there were 3,790 exclusions for racist abuse.

Shockingly there were also tens of thousands of cases of physical assault which led to expulsions, including 52,620 expulsions for pupils physically assaulting another pupil, and 17,680 expulsions for physical assault against an adult.

Mr Guy added: "School provides the perfect opportunity to improve life chances and help children fulfil their potential.

"It is alarming so many schools succumb to these problems which can have such a damaging and long-lasting impact."

The figures come from the Department of Education, and cover the latest recorded academic year, 2012/13. They relate to all state primary, secondary and special schools.

29 January 2015

⇨ The above information is reprinted with kind permission from the Centre for Social Justice. Please visit www.centreforsocialjustice.org.uk for further information.

Not my best career move!

More young people turning to teachers for drugs advice

Seven in ten 11- to-15-year-olds cite teachers as helpful sources of information on drugs, up since 2009.

A survey published today which was carried out by NatCen Social Research finds that 69% of 11- to 15-year-olds say that teachers are a helpful source of information about taking drugs, up from 63% in 2009. Almost as many pupils (68%) said their parents were also helpful sources.

However, young people today are less likely to think that their peers will give them helpful information about drugs; 42% mentioned friends and 33%, siblings.

The 2013 survey *Smoking, Drinking and Drug Use Among Young People in England* was carried out with 5,187 11- to 15-year-olds in 173 schools and explores pupils' experiences, beliefs and attitudes.

Between 2003 and 2011, drug use amongst 11- to 15-year-olds declined, but levels have stabilised over the last three years. In 2013, 16% of the age group said that they had tried at least one drug.

Could do better?

Even though teachers are seen as a key information source about drugs, a third of pupils would like to know more. Pupils were less likely to say that their school had given them enough information about drugs (66%) than about alcohol (70%) or smoking (73%).

And while more than four in five schools say that they provide lessons about smoking, drinking and drug use at least once a year, just three in five pupils recalled any such teaching in the last year.

TV tops other media

TV was consistently the most mentioned media source of helpful information about drugs over the last five years. In 2013, 59% of pupils mentioned TV as a source of helpful information about drugs, ahead of the Internet (53%). However, the impact of the government-funded website FRANK has fallen in recent years, from 36% in 2009 to 18% in 2013.

Elizabeth Fuller, Research Director at NatCen Social Research commented:

"The findings confirm the importance of teachers as a trusted and credible source for young people about drugs. However, there is still scope to improve. Fewer pupils than expected can recall receiving lessons about smoking, drinking and drug use, and a significant minority of young people still don't feel that their school gives them enough information about drugs."

24 July 2014

⇨ The above information is reprinted with kind permission from NatCen. Please visit www.natcen. ac.uk for further information.

Two million people misusing prescription drugs to get high, survey reveals

Almost two million people across England and Wales are abusing prescription painkillers either to get high or relax, according to a survey.

The Office for National Statistics (ONS) found more than 500,000 under-25s misused painkillers in the past year.

The painkillers being misused include codeine, morphine, tramadol and oxycodone, said the ONS crime survey of England and Wales.

This is the first time the annual study has asked about prescription-only painkillers and the question was included at the request of the Home Office.

Alistair Bohm, from Addaction, a charity for addiction, said there was growing evidence that painkiller misuse in the UK was a serious issue.

He said: "Most prescriptions are fully warranted, but should only ever be taken as instructed, as stronger opioids such as codeine or dihydrocodeine can be misused and lead to dependence.

"For many people though, painkillers are just one part of a more complex picture of drug use. They can be bought on the streets, through increasingly common online pharmacies or diverted from prescriptions and are also often used to supplement other drugs, like heroin," he added.

A report by DrugScope earlier this year found pregablin and gabapentin (used to treat epilepsy, pain or anxiety) were changing hands for as little as 50p a capsule for recreational use. Prisoners and opiate users were the main users of these drugs, said the *Street Drug Trend Survey*.

Home secretary, Theresa May has asked the Advisory Council on the Misuse of Drugs to investigate the abuse of prescription drugs. The report is due before 2016.

27 August 2015

⇨ The above information is reprinted with kind permission from *the Pharmacist*. Please visit www.thepharmacist.co.uk for further information.

Anabolic steroids a serious global health problem amid boom in cosmetic use

***An article from* The Conversation.**

By Dominic Sagoe, PhD Research Fellow in Social Psychology, University of Bergen

A competitive spirit is an indispensable aspect of human life, where it could be argued that a failure to compete only results in participating in a competition to fail. Over a very long period of time, humans have relied on various kinds of performance-enhancing substances. It has been suggested, for example, that the ancient Greeks turned to potions to improve performance.

Today, these substances range from 'soft' or legal substances such as energy drinks to 'hard' substances such as steroids and amphetamines, and other more 'natural' methods, including blood doping to increase the number of rich red blood cells in the bloodstream.

In the exercise or athletic world, anabolic-androgenic steroids or anabolic steroids are a very popular performance-enhancing substance. But over the past 40 years they have increasingly been used for aesthetic or 'beauty' reasons. This is what we found in a recent study, published in *Annals of Epidemiology*, that suggested that 3.3% of the world's population have used anabolic steroids at least once, most of whom were male (around 6.4% of males and 1.6% of females).

The biggest users were in the Middle East, followed by South America, Europe, North America, Oceania, Africa and Asia. Use was highest among recreational sportspeople followed by athletes, prisoners and arrestees, drug users, high school students and non-athletes.

Our finding suggests that use of anabolic steroids is now a serious global public health problem. Not confined to athletes, the spread of their use into the general population means millions of individuals across the world, many of whom have no athletic ambitions, are using them to increase and improve their physical strength and appearance.

A recent Australian survey suggested that two-thirds of young men who began injecting drugs in the past three years were using steroids (rather than methamphetamine or heroin).

Previous work

Anabolic steroids are a group of hormones that include the natural male sex hormone testosterone and a set of synthetic versions. Early scientific forays into the effects of testosterone included one Harvard professor injecting himself with a "rejuvenating elixir" that included extract from dog and guinea pig testicles in 1889. It wasn't until the mid-1930s, however, that human testosterone was first 'discovered' and then synthesised by Adolf Butenandt and Leopold Ruzicka (independently of each other) in 1939. Both were awarded the Nobel Prize for their work.

All anabolic steroids – natural and synthetic – have two essential results: a 'muscle-building' effect that results in muscle growth, and an androgenic or virilising effect that results in masculinising characteristics such as deepening of the voice. Anabolic steroids increase the production of protein within cells, which decreases body fat as well as increasing muscle growth beyond natural limits.

Steroids are used in medicine for several purposes including the treatment of male hypogonadism, a condition where the body doesn't produce enough testosterone and which can limit the production of sperm. It is also used to treat delayed puberty, enhance appetite and stimulate growth.

Many 'steroids' prescribed by medics are not anabolic, but corticosteroids which have neither anabolic nor addictive potential. But other people who use these steroids for fitness or aesthetic purposes clearly do it outside of these health reasons.

Spread to general population

Around the 1960s and 1970s, anabolic steroids were mainly used by elite athletes and bodybuilders motivated by the desire to develop bigger muscles and enhance their athletic performance. In the past three or four decades however, millions of non-competitive athletes such as recreational sportspeople and adolescents have been using them, motivated by the desire to look more attractive. This means their use has spread from the athletic community into the general population. While it has been suggested that athletes comprise the smallest group of anabolic users, in our study they were the second biggest.

Until recently, several questions over the global use estimates were largely unanswered. The aim of our study was to estimate the global prevalence of use. Putting together findings from 187 studies (and subject to some limitations such as the paucity of anabolic steroid prevalence research in especially Africa and Asia), we estimate the problem is gradually increasing. Between 1990 and 1999 prevalence was about 2.9% but post 2000, this has risen to 3.2%.

Harmful effects

These findings should attract the attention of global public health officials because of the associated serious harmful effects of long-term use. These include high blood pressure, heart attack, stroke, acne and skin infections, liver damage, tendon rupture, premature baldness, stunted bone growth in adolescents, syringe exchange infections such as HIV and hepatitis and death. There are psychosocial implications too. Users can become violent or aggressive, suffer mood syndromes, and addiction.

There are also other gender-specific effects. In males, these include low sperm count, shrunken testicles, infertility and growth of breasts. In females, these include roughening of the skin, decreased breast size, deepening of the voice, growth of body hair, changes to the menstrual cycle and enlargement of the clitoris.

It has to be noted that the effects and harms of anabolic use are dose-dependent. So higher and longer term use leads to bigger muscles but more harmful effects.

Laying down the law

Since the 1990s there has been increasing legislation to combat the problem. Anabolic steroid use is illegal in the US, the UK, Australia, Argentina, Brazil, Portugal and Saudi Arabia. Though the US passed their Anabolic Steroid Control Act in 1990, and Sweden the Act Prohibiting Certain Doping Substances in 1991, other countries have been a bit slower – Norway only banned use in 2013. In many places they are unregulated and can be bought in some pharmacies.

An amendment to the US act in 2004 also added prohormones to the list of controlled substances. These substances, a kind of precursor to a hormone (rather than a hormone itself), can amplify the effect of existing hormones.

But as the Internet makes obtaining substances easy, even if illegal, it's clear that better ways of dealing with the problem – and the probable harmful effect on population health – will need to be found.

13 March 2014

⇨ The above information is reprinted with kind permission from *The Conversation*. Please visit www. theconversation.com for further information.

Needle and syringe exchanges need to adapt to meet the needs of people who inject steroids and image-enhancing drugs

By Roger Pebody

The numbers of people injecting steroids and other image-enhancing drugs has increased significantly in the last decade and harm-reduction services need to develop new skills if they are to help people using these drugs avoid blood-borne viruses, the 24th International Harm Reduction Conference in Kuala Lumpur was told on Wednesday. Surveys in the United Kingdom suggest that rates of HIV and hepatitis infections are significantly higher in people using these drugs than in the general population.

Anabolic steroids are by far the most frequently used product, but agencies also report significant numbers of clients injecting peptide hormones, human growth hormone, and melanotan and other skin tanning agents. Collectively, they are variously referred to as steroids and image-enhancing drugs (SIEDs), performance and image-enhancing drugs (PIEDs), or image and performance-enhancing drugs (IPEDs).

The issue has been best documented in high-income countries (the conference presentations came from the UK and Australia), but some experts believe that this is likely to be a global phenomenon – for example, some of those using SIEDs in the UK were born in Eastern Europe and South-East Asia.

In both the UK and Australia, those using the substances are typically young men (around half are in their 20s). Most are heterosexual, but between 3% and 7% report sex with other men. Typically, they have limited experience of injecting drugs and tend not to use psychoactive drugs (except for cocaine, taken nasally). Nonetheless, both the UK and Australian surveys suggest that people using SIEDs are conscious of the risks of sharing equipment (4% and 2%, respectively had ever re-used another person's needle).

People using these drugs are described as being "thirsty for knowledge", but often seek this out on online forums where the information is not always accurate.

A higher than expected rate of HIV in people using SIEDs in the UK was first reported in 2013. In the most recent survey, 2% had HIV, 3% had antibodies to hepatitis B and 4% had antibodies to hepatitis C. It appears that the proportions with these infections have increased over time but the numbers taking part in surveys are small, so it is hard to be sure.

In contrast, in surveys of people using SIEDs in Queensland and New South Wales (Australia), 0.5% of people using SIEDs were HIV-positive. This is considerably higher than in the general heterosexual population of Australia (around 0.04%) but lower than among people injecting other drugs (2%) or gay men (8% to 12%). A larger number (5%) had antibodies to hepatitis C.

Given the elevated rate of HIV infection, the UK researchers argue that prevention work with people who use SIEDs needs to address sexual risks as well as injecting practices. In their surveys, around half of people who use SIEDs have multiple sexual partners but a similar proportion has never used a condom.

John Campbell of NHS Greater Glasgow and Clyde outlined how his needle and syringe programme had adapted to the needs of this group. The injecting equipment and techniques are distinct from those used by people who inject heroin, as steroids and image-enhancing drugs are injected into muscle or skin (rather than a vein).

A specialised service (one evening a week) has been mostly promoted through word of mouth recommendations. Black market steroid dealers have been more helpful in raising awareness of the service than the staff of local gyms.

Last year in the Greater Glasgow area, 3,339 individuals who injected SIEDs attended a needle exchange, in contrast to 7,670 who inject heroin. Whereas people who use heroin may attend several times a week, people who use steroids typically come in much less frequently. They usually pick up large quantities of equipment to cover a cycle of steroid use

and often take material to pass on to friends. The infrequent visits mean that these are relatively rare opportunities for education around safe use.

Advice is not limited to avoiding blood-borne viruses – many people have limited understanding of how the products work and what side-effects and harms they should expect. An important aspect of the service is to offer blood tests and give advice on the often abnormal kidney, liver, cholesterol, testosterone and oestrogen levels that a person may have.

In Australia, Jenny Iversen said that different states have taken different approaches. Queensland's policy on needle and syringe programmes explicitly states that people using SIEDs are a key group that the services must reach, with the aims of preventing new infections and of preventing injecting-related injuries. Educational materials for people using these products have been created.

In contrast, New South Wales – where the patterns of use of SIEDs are very similar – has chosen to limit the supply of equipment to this population, judging them not to be at sufficiently high risk of viral infections to warrant ongoing provision. Costs and a different

financial system to Queensland appear to be the main reason for the restrictions.

There is a "need for targeted harm reduction interventions to address the sexual health and drug use risks among those injecting image and performance-enhancing drugs," concluded Vivian Hope of Public Health England.

References

Cullen K et al. Risk and vulnerability among people who inject image and performance enhancing drugs in England and Wales 2012–2013: where should we focus harm reduction? 24th International Harm Reduction Conference, Kuala Lumpur, October 2015.

Iversen J and Maher L The harm reduction response to an increase in people who inject performance and image-enhancing drugs attending needle and syringe programmes in Australia: a tale of two states. 24th International Harm Reduction Conference, Kuala Lumpur, October 2015.

Campbell J and Hunter C Identifying and reducing harm for steroid and image enhancing drugs (SIEDs) injectors, through innovative approaches. 24th International Harm Reduction Conference, Kuala Lumpur, October 2015.

Hope VD et al. An increase in the prevalence of blood-borne infections among men who inject image and performance enhancing drugs in the United Kingdom: 1992–2013. 24th International Harm Reduction Conference, Kuala Lumpur, October 2015.

For harm reduction information on this issue, please visit www. ipedinfo.co.uk.

22 October 2015

⇨ The above information is reprinted with kind permission from aidsmap. Please visit www.aidsmap.com for further information.

Legal highs are no laughing matter say summer festival organisers

Legal highs on an all-time low? When the balloon goes up, it's no laughing matter...

On 1 April, Lincoln became the UK's first city to impose a complete ban on legal highs being used anywhere in public. Just one week later, five legal highs were banned by government drug advisers for 12 months to assess the harm posed.

Less than one month on comes the news that a 24-hour campaign to highlight the dangers of taking substances, such as nitrous oxide – known as 'laughing gas' – is to take place online, once again, this year.

Blacking out websites...

As the summer festival season gets underway, more than 40 venues, including Glastonbury, the Isle of Wight, Bestival, T in the Park, Lovebox and Parklife will be repeating last year's campaign action by blacking out their websites for 24 hours on Monday 4 May. Instead, the homepage of each festival site will show an infographic of 'key statistics, facts and advice on legal highs'.

The reality of legal highs today have long evolved from the chilled-out, plant-based 'herbal' alternatives to illegal drugs of summer festivals past. Ever since 'designer drugs' of the 1980s club scene, an explosion of new and unregulated, psychoactive compounds coming under the umbrella term of 'legal highs' have become commonly available – and posing risks even more lethal than traditional, illegal drugs. Designed to mimic the effects of ecstasy, cannabis and amphetamines, a high proportion are synthesised in China, India and across South-East Asia.

Alarming rise in deaths...

As a result of the new psychoactive substances, an alarming rise in the number of deaths began to be reported by The National Programme on Substance Abuse. Whilst there was ten deaths recorded in the UK in 2009, the

figure had jumped by more than fourfold to 42 deaths one year later and up by more than half again to 68 in 2012.

Over 100 new and unpredictable synthetic substances were recorded in 2014 by the European Monitoring Centre for Drugs and Drug Addiction (EMCDDA). As a result, the number of deaths linked to the use of legal highs has escalated eightfold in three years, according to the Centre for Social Justice (CSJ).

The same explosive pattern nationwide could be typically seen in microcosm, in Lincoln. The number of incidents involving legal highs in the city catapulted from seven to 820 between 2010 and 2014.

Of course the term 'legal highs' is not strictly true! An estimated 88 per cent of the legal highs are actually controlled and banned. The problem is the unstoppable influx of lethal new synthetic drugs, which are temporarily legal until the law catches up.

Aluminium canisters...

Highlighted recently has been the rising popularity and widespread use of nitrous oxide or 'laughing gas' among young clubbers and festival party goers, which continues to cause real health fears. Particularly popular among the younger crowd, more than one in 14 of those aged 16–24 used

nitrous oxide over a 12-month period, according to the Home Office with 17 deaths recorded between 2006 and 2012.

According to the Association of Independent Festivals, the deadly risks of legal highs were a "great concern to anyone involved in staging music festivals". However, it seemed that a 'blind eye' had been turned to nitrous oxide taking and the Home Office has asked summer festival organisers to ban the use of the substance, along with the introduction of a 'no legal highs' policy as a condition of entry to a festival site.

Veteran organisers, Glastonbury Festival have already declared that they will be banning nitrous oxide from their site this year. It now seems likely that many other festivals will also be keeping a beady eye out for little aluminium canisters and funny looking balloons...

May 2015

⇨ The above information is reprinted with kind permission from Help 4 Addiction. Please visit www.help4addiction.co.uk for further information.

'Legal highs' incidents up more than 150 per cent in a year, say police

The Centre for Social Justice has uncovered new data revealing the increasing damage 'legal highs' are having on society.

The number of police incidents involving 'legal highs' has almost trebled across England in a year, new figures obtained by the Centre for Social Justice (CSJ) reveal.

"The CSJ said the UK has the highest number of 'legal highs' users amongst young people in Europe"

Incidents soared across forces – from 1,356 in 2013 to 3,652 in 2014 (an increase of 169 per cent). But the overall number will be much higher as 12 of England's 39 police forces did not respond to the freedom of information request, including the Metropolitan Police.

In Greater Manchester the number increased 17-fold in two years, from six in 2012 – to 104 last year.

In West Yorkshire there was a 25-fold increase over the same period – from 13 to 324.

The CSJ has called for a robust response from the Government, including new police powers to close shops that persist in selling 'legal highs' (or New Psychoactive Substances).

This comes after recent CSJ analysis showed that the number of people in treatment for taking 'legal highs' jumped 216 per cent in England in the last five years.

The number of deaths associated with the use of 'legal highs' increased from 12 in 2009 to 97 in 2012 in the UK. In Scotland alone there were 113 deaths related to 'legal highs' in 2013.

"As well as posing worrying health risks, these figures suggest 'legal highs' are placing increasing pressure on public services," said former CSJ Director Christian Guy.

"The number of police incidents involving 'legal highs' has almost trebled across England in a year"

"It is too easy for young people to walk into high street shops and buy these drugs – many of them as dangerous and addictive as Class A substances.

"If we want to start responding to the problems caused by 'legal highs' we need to clamp down on those making a living out of selling them."

The CSJ said the UK has the highest number of 'legal highs' users amongst young people in Europe.

It has called for police and courts to be given new powers to close 'head shops' that sell many of the substances.

It wants the Government to implement legislation similar to a scheme run in Ireland, where authorities slashed the number of 'head shops' from more than 100 to less than ten within a month.

9 February 2015

⇨ The above information is reprinted with kind permission from The Centre For Social Justice. Please visit www.centreforsocialjustice.org.uk for further information.

IT'S OKAY – IT'S LEGAL!

Drugs and the law

Each illegal drug is put into a different 'class'. The law on drugs is complex. But if you're caught with an illegal substance, ignorance won't wash with the police. Here's what you need to know.

Illegal drugs are divided into different 'classes' by the Misuse of Drugs Act. If you're caught with drugs, the punishment you'll get depends on what class the drug is. You'll also face different punishments depending on whether you were just in possession of it, or if you intended to supply it to others.

What different classes of drugs are there?

Class A

⇨ Cocaine, crack, crystal meth, ecstasy, heroin, LSD (acid), magic mushrooms, mephadone and any class B drug prepared for injection.

⇨ Maximum penalties: seven years in prison and/or a fine for possession, life imprisonment and/or a fine for possession with intent to supply.

Class B

⇨ Amphetamines (speed), cannabis, codeine.

⇨ Maximum penalties: five years in prison and/or a fine for possession, 14 years in prison and/or a fine for possession with intent to supply.

Class C

⇨ Ketamine, some tranquillisers like Temazepam, the supply of anabolic steroids.

⇨ Maximum penalties: two years in prison and/or a fine for possession, 14 years prison and/or a fine for possession with intent to supply.

These penalties are given in a Crown Court. In a Magistrates Court, where less serious offences are dealt with, the maximum sentence is six months imprisonment and a £5,000 fine. The actual sentence you're likely to get will also depend on:

⇨ The drug involved;

⇨ Any previous criminal record;

⇨ Your personal circumstances (i.e. being a single parent);

⇨ The attitude of the presiding magistrate/judge.

Some other drugs are controlled by the Medicines Act. It may not be illegal to possess drugs such as prescription medicines, but supply is still an offence.

Other drug laws

Most drugs are covered by the Misuse of Drugs Act. These ones aren't:

⇨ **Alcohol:** There are lots of laws about alcohol, covering where it can be sold, who to and where you can drink it.

⇨ **Solvents:** It is not illegal to use, but a shopkeeper can be prosecuted for selling a solvent to under-18s who they know will use it for sniffing.

⇨ **Cigarettes:** It is illegal for a shopkeeper to knowingly sell to under-18s;

⇨ **Amyl nitrates (poppers):** Amyl nitrate is a prescription-only medicine. Possession is not an offence, but supply is restricted by the Medicines Act. Butyl and Isobutyl nitrate are not restricted in any way. The stuff available from jokes and sex shops is usually butyl or isobutyl nitrate. If any amyl nitrate is present, however, then supply is restricted. Use is not.

From some time in 2016, the Psychoactive Substances Act will come into force. This act will not replace the Misuse of Drugs Act (1971), but it will make it an offence to produce or supply legal highs. It won't be an offence to possess them.

The above information is reprinted with kind permission from The Mix – Essential support for under 25s (www.themixuk.org).

TheMixUK.org is the guide to life for under 25-year-olds in the UK. We provide non-judgmental support and information on everything from sex and exam stress to debt and drugs.

*Our straight-talking emotional support is available 24 hours a day. On TheMixUK.org you can: * Chat about anything you like on our moderated discussion boards and live chat room.*

* Browse over 2,000 articles and videos full of facts you can trust.

* Read about the experiences of other young people in our True Life section.

* Call us free on 0808 808 4994 (every day 11am–11pm).

Legalising drugs would bring not freedom but enslavement

Pro-drug liberals are blind to the side-effects of their theories. Most parents do not want their children exposed to such an experiment.

By Kathy Gyngell

From the relentless pro-drugs legalisation media blitz of the last few weeks, you would think this was the most pressing item on the Government's agenda after the floods. It is not. Who is behind this campaign with a Gantt chart on their wall logging the daily media hits is a question for another day.

My worry is why responsible people are lending their names to this 'cause' when they are so obviously ignorant of the facts and the implications. I am not bothered about Russell Brand. His petition demanding a parliamentary debate has become the stuff of comedy, given his earlier public strictures on ignoring democracy. Beyond celebrity groupies and metropolitan admirers, his erratic and self-serving ramblings won't persuade.

No, the people who perturb me are middle-aged political converts to this cause: Nick Clegg, Nigel Farage, Daniel Hannan and Norman Fowler. Whether intentionally or not, they have aligned themselves in a culture war which pits the liberal against traditionalist, cosmopolitan against parochial and old against young. This is what drugs' legalisation is about: a war over fundamental values. It is not a battle about basic freedoms – far from it. Drugs enslave.

I doubt whether any of these politicians are or were 'recreational' drug users, let alone former addicts, or that they'd wish drugs on their children. Yet they've been persuaded that a hypothetical taxed and regulated system – one they've been told would cut police and prison costs, undercut criminal gangs and end the war on drugs to boot – would sanitise drug use. It wouldn't; it would normalise it.

Hannan, the normally sceptical Conservative MEP, is the most recent convert. "Do you want your children to take drugs?" is the wrong question to ask, he says. Many would beg to disagree. Having dispensed with children, the crux of his case is that "most quantitative analyses conclude that [drug] legalisation would bring net advantages".

He is right that a number of economic analyses commissioned and published by pro-drugs lobby groups claim this by computing the fiscal costs associated with existing laws. He is wrong if he thinks they address and estimate the full costs of legalisation. Quite simply, the data required for a formal cost-benefit analysis is not available.

As the authors of the report that so impressed him admit, theirs are "subjective indications... some of which should be regarded as illustrative calculations rather than formal estimates".

The social and economic costs of departing from current policy – whether bearing on public health, mental health, education, productivity or crime (including drug driving) policing, wide-scale drug testing or bureaucracy – are

Proportion of 16- to 59-year-olds reporting use of Class A drugs ever in their lifetime, 2005–2014/15

	2005/06	2006/07	2007/08	2008/09	2009/10	2010/11	2011/12	2012/13	2013/14	2014/15
Class A										
Any cocaine	7.4	7.8	7.8	9.3	8.7	8.9	9.6	8.9	9.5	9.8
Powder cocaine	7.3	7.7	7.7	9.2	8.6	8.8	9.4	8.8	9.4	9.7
Crack cocaine	0.9	1.0	0.9	1.0	1.2	1.2	1.3	1.0	1.0	1.2
Ecstasy	7.3	7.4	7.6	8.6	8.3	8.3	8.6	8.3	9.3	9.2
Hallucinogens	9.5	9.2	9.1	9.4	9.2	9.2	9.2	9.0	9.1	8.5
LSD	5.6	5.5	5.3	5.5	5.3	5.3	5.4	5.1	5.3	4.7
Magic mushrooms	7.4	7.2	7.0	7.5	7.4	7.2	7.5	7.2	7.3	7.1
Opiates	0.9	0.8	0.8	0.9	0.9	0.9	1.1	0.8	1.1	0.9
Heroin	0.7	0.7	0.7	0.7	0.7	0.6	0.8	0.6	0.8	0.7
Methadone	0.5	0.4	0.4	0.4	0.4	0.6	0.7	0.5	0.6	0.6

Source: Drug misuse: findings from 2014/15 Crime Survey for England and Wales, Appendix Tables

all unknowns. Estimates of increased use vary between 75% and 289% after legalisation, more if advertising is permitted.

Invoking fiscal rhetoric to advance legalisation – like Hannan's frankly barmy call for a temporary 12-month suspension of the drugs laws, starting with cannabis – is not just deceitful, it is downright irresponsible.

I can only assume that he is unaware of the consequences of Brixton's cannabis decriminalisation experiment and of the later temporary nationwide declassification of cannabis. I guess he does not know that immediate rises in consumption of 25% and 30% took place, nor how long it took for analysis of this to reach the public domain.

I doubt he knows of Kelly and Rasul's [2013] testing of the wider impact of the Brixton experiment. Their key finding was a dramatic rise in hospital admissions of 15- to 34-year-old Class A drug users. They were 40-100% more likely to be admitted during the policy trial – a period in which police were sanctioned to ignore street-level cannabis offences.

But like the pro-legalising thinktank head I sat next to at dinner recently, I suspect Hannan's grasp of the drug problem is pretty limited. My dinner companion had no idea how marginal an activity drug use is compared with smoking and drinking – living as he does among London's metropolitan liberals.

He was surprised that fewer than 3% of adults smoke a spliff at all regularly compared with the 20% who smoke daily and the overwhelming majority who regularly drink alcohol. He had no idea that cannabis use overall had declined in the UK, and so markedly amongst adolescents – 30% in the last 15 years.

He was unaware that over the same period in the United States, when 21 states legalised so-called medical marijuana, teenage drug use doubled to much higher levels than here and was accompanied by a halving of teens' perception of harm. He knew little of the greatly enhanced cancer risks of smoking cannabis, its effects on the adolescent brain – on motivation, IQ, psychosis and schizophrenia – or that cannabis as a coroner-noted cause of death, although limited, is increasing.

He rolled out the same old cliché as did Hannan: that it would be preferable, if children are to do drugs, they do them safely – quality controlled from Boots without a dealer in sight, of course, and never mind their age. Not even Professor Nutt personally handing them out would make it safe, I pointed out, not after they've downed several vodkas and already raided their parent's newly legal supply at home.

No matter, in their brave new world, taxation on all that pot not grown at home, and not leaked onto the illicit market, will pay for the damage done to the next generation. The irony is that Hannan and his fellow libertarians may soon find themselves on the wrong side of the culture war.

For today's young people are more, not less, responsible than before: they drink less, use drugs less, commit fewer crimes and volunteer more, as a recent Demos report shows. In these newly competitive times, the last thing this generation need is a drugs-legalising experiment foisted on them by ageing libertarians.

Anyway, there already is one – in Colorado. It does not look good. According to Dr Christian Thurstone, the director of one of Colorado's largest youth substance-abuse treatment clinics, regular high school drug use has leaped from 19% to 30% since Colorado legalised medical marijuana in 2009 for adults; teens are using more higher potency products; school expulsions are up by a third, and 74% of teens in his drug-treatment clinic are using somebody else's medical marijuana, all of it diverted through somebody who is 18 or older.

Since full legalisation the school situation in Colorado has got worse. "Kids are smoking before school and during lunch breaks. They come into school reeking of pot," school resource officers say. "Students don't seem to realise that there is anything wrong with having the pot… they act like having marijuana was an ordinary thing and no big deal".

Hannan might not mind exposing his children to this experiment. I think most parents would.

This article originally appeared on ConservativeHome.

20 February 2014

⇨ The above information is reprinted with kind permission from *The Guardian*. Please visit www.theguardian.com for further information.

Drugs penalties

The penalties depend on which drug and the amount you have, and whether you are also dealing or producing the drug. The most severe penalty can be an unlimited fine and life in prison.

Types of drugs

The maximum penalties for drug possession, supply (dealing) and production depend on what type or 'class' the drug is.

Possessing drugs

You may be charged with possessing an illegal substance if you're caught with drugs, whether they're yours or not.

If you're under 18, the police are allowed to tell your parent, guardian or carer that you've been caught with drugs.

Your penalty will depend on:

⇨ the class and quantity of drug

⇨ where you and the drugs were found

⇨ your personal history (previous crimes, including any previous drug offences)

⇨ other aggravating or mitigating factors.

Cannabis

Police can issue a warning or an on-the-spot fine of £90 if you're found with cannabis.

Khat

Police can issue a warning or an on-the-spot fine of £60 on the first 2 times that you're found with khat. If you're found with khat more than twice, you could get a maximum penalty of up to two years in prison, an unlimited fine, or both.

Dealing or supplying drugs

The penalty is likely to be more severe if you are found to be supplying or dealing drugs. Sharing drugs is also considered supplying.

Class	Drug	Possession	Supply and production
A	Crack cocaine, cocaine, ecstasy (MDMA), heroin, LSD, magic mushrooms, methadone, methamphetamine (crystal meth)	Up to seven years in prison, an unlimited fine or both	Up to life in prison, an unlimited fine or both
B	Amphetamines, barbiturates, cannabis, codeine, ketamine, methylphenidate (Ritalin), synthetic cannabinoids, synthetic cathinones (e.g. mephedrone, methoxetamine)	Up to five years in prison, an unlimited fine or both	Up to 14 years in prison, an unlimited fine or both
C	Anabolic steroids, benzodiazepines (diazepam), gamma hydroxybutyrate (GHB), gamma-butyrolactone (GBL), piperazines (BZP), khat	Up to two years in prison, an unlimited fine or both (except anabolic steroids - it's not an offence to possess them for personal use)	Up to 14 years in prison, an unlimited fine or both
Temporary class drugs*	Some methylphenidate substances (3,4-dichloromethylphenidate (3,4-DCMP), methylnaphthidate (HDMP-28), isopropylphenidate (IPP or IPPD), 4-methylmethylphenidate, ethylnaphthidate, propylphenidate) and their simple derivatives	None, but police can take away a suspected temporary class drug	Up to 14 years in prison, an unlimited fine or both

*The government can ban new drugs for one year under a 'temporary banning order' while they decide how the drugs should be classified.

The police will probably charge you if they suspect you of supplying drugs. The amount of drugs found and whether you have a criminal record will affect your penalty.

⇨ The above information is reprinted with kind permission from GOV.UK.

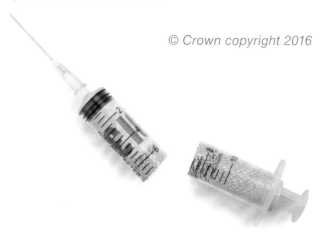

Drug policy is working – why do we prefer to think otherwise?

An article from The Conversation.

THE CONVERSATION

By Paul Hayes

On all sides, our politicians and commentators seem convinced Britain's drug policy has been a failure.

Party conference season saw Liberal Democrat leader Nick Clegg rehash his old refrain that we've "lost the war on drugs". Iain Duncan Smith's Centre for Social Justice still portrays drug addiction as one of the main drivers of worklessness, poverty and social exclusion in our poorest communities. And on 30 October, the narrative of failure will be rehearsed yet again when Green MP Caroline Lucas initiates a three-hour debate in Parliament calling for an impact assessment of our current drug laws.

But these diagnoses are misleading: for all the problems that remain, the major successes of our drug policy deserve to be acknowledged. Here are some of the headline facts, which can take even informed observers by surprise.

Turning it around

Drug use is much less common than most people assume. In England and Wales, about one adult in three will have used a drug in their lifetime; for the vast majority, this will be short-term or intermittent cannabis use.

Use of the most dangerous drug, heroin, is much rarer. Public Health England estimate there are now fewer than 300,000 heroin users in England, compared to estimates of more than 450,000 at the height of the heroin epidemic in 1999.

The biggest fall in heroin use has been among young people; our addiction problem is in a cohort of middle-aged users, who began using heroin in the 1980s and 1990s and who also suffer from poor mental health, alcohol misuse, homelessness and social exclusion. By and large, they are not the vulnerable teenagers of popular imagination.

Meanwhile, a range of research suggests that a major part of the sharp rise in crime experienced in the 1980s and 1990s was caused by the dramatic increase in heroin use during that period; it is also estimated that ready access to treatment (including in prison) currently prevents 4.9 million crimes per year.

Levels of HIV, closely associated with needle injection around the world, are also very low among British injectors, largely thanks to the harm-reduction policies pioneered by Norman Fowler when he was Margaret Thatcher's Health secretary in the 1980s. In the USA, up to 20% of injectors have HIV; in Byisk, in Russia, it's more than 70%. But in England, the rate is just over 2%.

Of course, not all the news is good. Drug-related deaths rose startlingly in 2013, after falling each year since 2010. The immediate and long-term health risks of 'legal highs' are still poorly understood; the poor integration of drug and mental health services is a continuing scandal.

But if we resist the meaningless rhetoric of 'winning' or 'losing' the 'war on drugs', we'll see that the broader reality of England's drug problem today is that fewer people are using drugs, fewer are becoming addicted and the social and economic impacts of drug use are shrinking.

> **Drug use is lower than it was ten years ago:**
>
> 8.6% in 2014/15 vs. 11.2% in 2004/05 among 16- to 50-year-olds*

We've clearly come a long way since the first national drug strategy, Tackling Drugs Together. While drug addiction still has a disproportionate impact on vulnerable citizens living in Britain's poorest communities, there is no longer a plausible argument that drug addiction is destabilising our society.

Yet despite rapidly declining use, falling crime, an ageing cohort of users as young people shun heroin and still-low levels of HIV – all of which would once have been seen as causes of celebration and proof of success – British drug policy is almost universally derided as a failure. Why?

Decline and fall

For ideologues of a traditionalist conservative bent, drug use is part of a broader liberal folly, a social programme that has trashed the morals – self-reliance, responsibility, deferred gratification, sacrifice, duty – that

* Source: Findings from the 2014/15 Crime Survey for England and Wales

supposedly characterised family and social life across all classes before the social upheaval of the 1960s.

To accept that drug use has been falling for years and that its attendant harms are clearly in retreat would destroy this dystopian vision. It would also invite a less politically convenient explanation for poverty, one that emphasises structural inequality rather than the individual failings of the poor. Faced with this prospect, the easier option for ideologues is to ignore the facts, thereby sustaining the integrity of their analysis and the power of their polemic.

Meanwhile, the liberal intelligentsia apparently sees recreational drug use as relatively benign, chalking all harm up to the consequences of prohibition and the "failed war on drugs". Prohibition is blamed for the mass incarceration of young black men in the USA and the deaths of thousands in Mexico's drug wars, as well as providing a justification for continuing US interference in supposedly sovereign Central and South American states.

These arguments usually conclude with a call to review the 1971 Misuse of Drugs Act, as if that's the prime cause of racism in the US justice system, explains the history of US-Latin American relations, or drives the brutal internecine struggles of the Mexican cartels.

But given the reality of the situation, an honest discussion of the real situation in Britain – less use, less harm, ready access to treatment – would hardly support a wholesale review of drug laws and the UN convention.

Running riot

Across the commentariat, opinions on drugs are a means to signal political identity and affiliation. The brand value of being in favour of either legalisation or prohibition is much too potent to allow it to be diminished by inconvenient truths.

The real public health and crime crises that followed in the wake of the heroin epidemic spawned

an evidence-based cross-party consensus that still underpins the policies in place today. And it is that same success that has freed the ideologues from the necessity to engage with messy reality and let them loose in an anarchic ideological playground.

Flagrant ideological posturing along these lines flourishes in our nonsensically combative political culture. It's almost impossible for any government policy to be called a success; politicians have learned that to claim a win for any policy is to invite a charge of complacency today and risk humiliation tomorrow.

The resulting fixation on problems, failures and misfires drives any genuine improvement so far down the agenda that it falls out of sight. In Whitehall, political invisibility means being starved of cash and influence – and this creates a dynamic in which civil servants, producer interests and service users learn to displace good news with a constantly evolving narrative of failure.

Get real

There are obviously legitimate debates to be had about how we protect the public from the harms of illegal drugs – and the role of criminal sanctions. On the one hand, is it morally justifiable to lock people up for possession to protect them from themselves? On the other, under a more liberal

regime, how would we stop a free market driving up both use and harm?

These are not easy questions to answer, and they demand a proper debate. But as things stand, our absurd ignorance of our own success means we're drifting towards unnecessarily radical 'solutions' – even though it's entirely possible to develop incremental improvements to our management of illegal drugs to sit alongside our responses to alcohol and legal highs.

The stale, ideological alternatives our political tribes are still pushing would scarcely be contemplated if the successes of our current policy got a tenth as much airplay as its problems do. And the losers from this will not be publicity-hungry entrepreneurs or misguided think-tankers, but rather the 0.5% of our population for whom drug policy is genuinely a matter of life and death.

30 October 2014

⇨ The above information is reprinted with kind permission from *The Conversation*. Please visit www.theconversation.com for further information.

Drugs and driving: the law

It's illegal to drive if either:

⇨ you're unfit to do so because you're on legal or illegal drugs

⇨ you have certain levels of illegal drugs in your blood (even if they haven't affected your driving).

Legal drugs are prescription or over-the-counter medicines. If you're taking them and not sure if you should drive, talk to your doctor, pharmacist or healthcare professional.

The police can stop you and make you do a 'field impairment assessment' if they think you're on drugs. This is a series of tests, e.g. asking you to walk in a straight line. They can also use a roadside drug kit to screen for cannabis and cocaine.

If they think you're unfit to drive because of taking drugs, you'll be arrested and will have to take a blood or urine test at a police station.

You could be charged with a crime if the test shows you've taken drugs.

Prescription medicines

It's illegal in England and Wales to drive with legal drugs in your body if it impairs your driving.

It's an offence to drive if you have over the specified limits of certain drugs in your blood and you haven't been prescribed them.

Talk to your doctor about whether you should drive if you've been prescribed any of the following drugs:

⇨ amphetamine, e.g. dexamphetamine or selegiline

⇨ clonazepam

⇨ diazepam

⇨ flunitrazepam

⇨ lorazepam

⇨ methadone

⇨ morphine or opiate and opioid-based drugs, e.g. codeine, tramadol or fentanyl

⇨ oxazepam

⇨ temazepam.

You can drive after taking these drugs if:

⇨ you've been prescribed them and followed advice on how to take them by a healthcare professional

⇨ they aren't causing you to be unfit to drive even if you're above the specified limits.

You could be prosecuted if you drive with certain levels of these drugs in your body and you haven't been prescribed them.

The law doesn't cover Northern Ireland and Scotland but you could still be arrested if you're unfit to drive.

Penalties for drug driving

If you're convicted of drug driving you'll get:

⇨ a minimum one year driving ban

⇨ an unlimited fine

⇨ up to six months in prison

⇨ a criminal record.

Your driving licence will also show you've been convicted for drug driving. This will last for 11 years.

The penalty for causing death by dangerous driving under the influence of drugs is a prison sentence of up to 14 years.

Other problems you could face

A conviction for drug driving also means:

⇨ your car insurance costs will increase significantly

⇨ if you drive for work, your employer will see your conviction on your licence

⇨ you may have trouble travelling to countries like the USA.

4 August 2015

⇨ The above information is reprinted with kind permission from GOV.UK.

> Whatever gave you the idea I'm under the influence?

Detox or lose your benefits: new welfare proposals are based on bad evidence and worse ethics

An article from **The Conversation.**

THE CONVERSATION

By Ian Hamilton, Lecturer in Mental Health, University of York

When is a choice not really a choice? It could be argued that the latest proposal from the Government aimed at people who have problems with drugs and alcohol is not a choice but an ultimatum – accept help for your problem or lose your right to welfare benefits.

This proposal raises some very serious issues. Treating any condition is based on consent – the person should be willing to have the treatment. In this case, people have little choice and therefore they would probably be consenting to treatment to avoid losing money. This also passes on an ethical dilemma to treatment staff, who would need to decide if they are willing to participate in state-sponsored coercion.

The consultation on these issues, led by Carol Black, will have its supporters. The Government has pledged to reduce the country's deficit. When tax-payers' money is given to people who will inevitably spend some of it on the substances they are reliant on, many people despair. The idea of sanctioning addicts will resonate broadly with the public who often view drug and alcohol problems as self-inflicted in the first place. But that is not the full story – and to cut through these emotionally charged arguments we need to consider the context.

The first thing to consider is how many people who have drug and alcohol problems claim welfare benefits – something that, unfortunately, we don't know. Even the Government's own recently published calculations of those in treatment and claiming benefit are three years out of date. It is clear that the results of the consultation will inform the Treasury spending review which is due to report in November. But if we don't how many people are claiming benefits and are

not in contact with treatment services, it is difficult to see how this review will be based on anything other than guesswork. This is not the finest hour for the new era of evidence-based policy.

Compounding this missing data is the lack of proof supporting such an initiative. There is already good evidence from other parts of the world that coercive treatment does not produce the desired benefits It would be naïve to assume that people only have problems with drugs and alcohol. Most will have a range of complex and interrelated issues in which their physical and mental health is also compromised. This complexity is not matched by a sophisticated system of treatment. Services have become increasingly specialised and resistant to accepting people who don't meet their strict criteria. Navigating such complex pathways into and around treatment would challenge the most cognitively able.

Treatment can take time and, for most people, will require more than one attempt to recover from addiction. So if drug treatment becomes compulsory, the capacity of treatment services will need attention. Particularly if funding for drug treatment continues to be cut, then the capacity of these services to accept the increasing number of referrals will be compromised. This initiative could also make it more difficult for those who are ready for treatment to access services. Increasing demand without resources to match will delay entry into treatment for many.

If the moral arguments for treatment fail to seduce politicians and taxpayers perhaps the clear economic case might be persuasive. For every £1 invested there is a conservative estimate that £9 is saved by reducing crime and other health costs.

In economically austere times, led by a government that believes it has a mandate to cut public costs, we need to be realistic about what form drug and alcohol support takes, ask whether there's evidence to justify it and think carefully about the unintended consequences.

These are challenging times for people who have problems with addiction, and those who wish to help them. We must speak up quickly and with one voice. Not only to challenge the ideology of this review but to offer some fresh views of our own.

3 August 2015

⇨ The above information is reprinted with kind permission from *The Conversation*. Please visit www.theconversation.com for further information.

Drug laws around the world – does anyone get it right?

As a split emerges in the Government over Britain's future drug policy we look at the different approaches to drug control taken around the world.

By Georgia Graham

The Coalition Government is at war over a new report which suggests that decriminalising drugs could have benefits to the UK.

The Home Office report examining a range of approaches, from zero-tolerance to decriminalisation, concluded drug use was influenced by factors "more complex and nuanced than legislation and enforcement alone".

The Conservatives say despite the Home Office-backed study indicating that decriminalising drugs, even class A substances such as heroin and cocaine, could have some benefits by reducing the burden on the criminal justice system the Government has "absolutely no plans" to decriminalise drugs.

The Liberal Democrats argue that punishing drug users is "pointless" with Lib Dem Home Office minister Norman Baker accusing No.10 of sitting on the reports since July and blamed the Conservatives for blocking their release for "political reasons".

It is not just British parties that are split over how to tackle drug use - countries across the world take very different approaches from decriminalisation to lengthy prison sentences and even death. Does anyone get it right?

Portugal

A large part of the report focused on Portugal where drugs were effectively decriminalised over ten years ago. According to the Home Office analysis there has been a "considerable" improvement in the health of drug users in Portugal since the country made drug possession a health issue rather than a criminal one in 2001.

In 2000, Portugal decriminalised the use of all illicit drugs, and developed new policies on prevention, treatment, harm reduction and reinsertion. Drug use is no longer a crime, but it is still prohibited. The country's policy was a key comparison in the report written by Home Office civil servants.

Possession of what a person would use in ten days or less is no longer a matter for the courts. Users are referred to 'Commissions for Drug Addiction Dissuasion' where they are given treatment.

Over the last decade the approach appears to have worked in the country, with João Castel-Branco Goulão Portugal's national drug coordinator saying the country has seen reductions in HIV infections and in overdoses.

So what about the rest of the world?

Czech Republic

Similarly to Portugal, possession of drugs is illegal, but possession of small quantities treated as an 'administrative offence', punishable with a fine.

Unlike Portugal, levels of cannabis use in the Czech Republic are among the highest in Europe.

While criminal penalties for possession were only introduced as recently as 2010 the report concluded that worse health outcomes were observed after drug possession was criminalised, and there was no evidence of reduced use.

Uruguay

In 2013 Uruguay became the first country in the world to full legalise marijuana. It is now the first nation in the world to break the International Convention on Drug Control, and legislate for the production, sale and consumption of cannabis.

Ten per cent of the country's prison population was for small drug offences – and 44 per cent of all drugs cases were for people detained for holding less than 10g of drugs.

Uruguayans will now be allowed to by up to 40g a month from pharmacies, join a cannabis club which grows the plant for its members grow up to six plants themselves.

The Government here says the change in the law is an effort to separate the marijuana market from more problematic drug use. This includes the smoking of 'pasta base' – a cheap derivative of cocaine that is highly addictive when smoked and has become endemic in some poor communities.

However the Uruguayan President Jose Mujica has said the start of legal cannabis sales will be delayed until next year due to "practical difficulties".

The Netherlands

Famously a tourist hot-spot for people seeking cannabis from countries with stricter controls, substances defined as 'soft' drugs, including cannabis, have been effectively decriminalised. Possession remains illegal here but police and courts operate a policy of tolerance.

The reported number of deaths linked to the use of drugs in The Netherlands, as a proportion of the entire population, is one of the lowest of the EU. Attempts to crack down on the use of cannabis by tourists have been widely ignored in the country.

However, importing and exporting of any classified drug is a serious offence. The penalty can run up to 12 to 16 years if it is for hard drugs with a maximum of four years for importing or exporting large quantities of cannabis.

Japan

Japan has the toughest drug laws in the developed world. Its Pharmaceutical Affairs Law bans the production and sale of 68 types of drugs and has a zero-tolerance policy. Criminal sanctions are tougher than in the UK and relatively few people seek treatment.

Some products that are available over the counter as cold and flu remedies are banned and possession of even small amounts of drugs is punishable by lengthy imprisonment.

There are low levels of drug use in Japan but the report notes that it is difficult to decide whether this can be attributed to harsh penalties or a long cultural opposition to drugs and a society where cultural conformity is valued.

USA

In 2012, states in the US – Washington State and Colorado – have legalised the recreational use of cannabis, putting them in direct conflict with President Obama's national drug policy.

18 states and the District of Columbia allow the use of medical marijuana on prescription.

However, in Colorado aged over 21 are to be allowed to buy and possess up to an ounce (28g) of cannabis and grow six plants in a private, secure area. The first $25 million raised through taxes on these sales will go towards the building of schools.

In Washington, licenses to sell marijuana are issued by the state alcohol control boards and the number of outlets are limited. They can't be within 1,000 feet of a school, playground or library.

China

Drug possession for personal use is technically classified as a minor administrative offence but punishment can be harsh – a 2,000 RMB fine and up to 15 days of administrative detention.

The Government can also send people who are deemed to be drug addicts to a compulsory detoxification centre for up to three years, plus up to three years' compulsory "community rehabilitation".

In 2013, Guangdong province in the south launched the 'Thunder Anti-drug' special action. 97,200 drug users were detained and 47,400 people were sent to compulsory detoxification centres.

Smuggling or transporting or manufacturing 1,000 grams or more of opium and 50 grams of more of heroin can lead to a death sentence.

According to the most recent figures in 2008 there were 1,126,700 registered drug users, 900,000 were using heroin or other opioids.

Ireland

While it has a similar drugs policy to the UK, Ireland has been the leading the way on the control of 'legal highs'. In 2010 the country banned all 'psychoactive' substances unless specific exemptions are made, as is the case with tea, coffee and alcohol.

Denmark

The country has recently followed the example of The Netherlands and Germany and opened 'fix rooms' for serious drug addicts where they can safely consume and inject drugs in a supervised environment.

The facilities are on offer to adults with serious addictions who can bring their illegal drugs and take them, legally, under the watchful eye of a nurse. The capital Copenhagen opened the first with other cities following suit.

Sweden

Sweden is seen as the toughest zero-tolerance state with regards to drugs in Western Europe.

Both use and possession are illegal. Even minor use can lead to a prison sentence of six months although more generally leads to a fine.

The United Nations Office on Drugs and Crime (UNODC) reports that Sweden has one of the lowest drug usage rates in the Western world, and attributes this to a drug policy that invests heavily in prevention and treatment as well as strict law enforcement.

Although praised by those who back the 'war on drugs' approach for its low level of cannabis use of harder drugs is a very high proportion of drug use.

Drug treatment is free of charge and provided through the health care system and the municipal social services.

30 October 2014

⇨ The above information is reprinted with kind permission from *The Telegraph*. Please visit www.telegraph.co.uk for further information.

Let's end the war on drugs by making them legal

By Ian Bell

It could be a pub quiz question. What do Armenia and Argentina have in common? The Czech Republic and Chile? Paraguay and Poland? The answer isn't football. Each has decided, in some fashion, that if you just say no to drugs, you say nothing useful at all.

Depending on the definitions used, there are between 25 and 30 such countries. Their laws, methods, aims and ambitions vary. Some have legalised drugs. Some have 're-legalised'. A few never got around to prohibition to begin with. Most have experimented – for personal use, you understand – with a gateway policy, decriminalisation.

Last week the Republic of Ireland decided, in effect, that what's good enough for Belgium, Spain, Portugal, Estonia, The Netherlands and others might help with its own liberation from the half-century of failure we still call, without irony, the war on drugs. With a leaked report suggesting that the UN Office on Drugs and Crime (UNODC) is on the brink of advocating decriminalisation, Ireland joins a growing consensus.

Britain doesn't want to hear about that. Or rather, the Conservative Government doesn't want to hear the accusation "soft on drugs" from its press sponsors. Amid a fragrant haze of hypocrisy, the line is that there will be no change, funding cuts aside, in UK drugs strategy. Meanwhile, police forces the length of these islands are improvising policies of their own.

In Ireland, serious thinking has been going on. The result, if carried through, will be the decriminalisation of drugs in personal use quantities combined with the introduction of injection (consumption) rooms. Narcotics will remain illegal, but in future – or such is the hope – no-one will be treated as a criminal because of an addiction or a problematic habit. The Irish are making a fundamental distinction.

Officially, Britain remains tough, tougher than tough, on drugs. Unofficially, an ad hoc pragmatism guides enforcement. A fall of close to a third in cannabis possession offences in England and Wales between 2011–12 and 2014–15 has not happened because dope has lost its allure. With budgets cut to ribbons, police forces have concluded they have better things to do than harass cannabis users.

There are worse principles a government could apply. In a speech at the London School of Economics last Monday, Aodhain O'Riordain, the Irish minister responsible for drugs strategy, maintained that a "cultural shift" is required. Addiction should be regarded as a health issue, he argued, both for the sake of individuals and for the benefit of law enforcement. Time and money spent hunting addicts could be better used against a criminal trade.

O'Riordain advocates de-criminalisation, not legalisation. He is not alone in that, though at the LSE he failed to explain the logic. Portugal's experience over the last 14 years is the Irish minister's inspiration, as it is for many reluctant conscripts in the war on drugs, but a conspicuous Iberian success remains half an answer to a complicated question.

With Europe's highest HIV infection rate among injecting drugs users, Portugal faced an undoubted crisis at the turn of the century. Desperate, it decided that drug use or possession should remain offences, but not criminal offences. The money spent on treatment and prevention was doubled. The police meanwhile began to ignore mere marijuana use. And the HIV rate started to fall.

It has not been plain sailing since. According to some studies, hard drug use has increased. More people have sought treatment, perhaps as a result, but the number of drug-related deaths has declined. Pressure on courts has eased, meanwhile, and the street price of drugs has fallen. Adolescent use seems to be waning, but with the police still seizing several tonnes of cocaine each year, the effect of reform on organised crime has been hard to measure.

That, though, is an aspect of decriminalisation too often overlooked. On its own, without a wider health policy or O'Riordain's "person-centred" strategy, it does not 'solve' a narcotics problem. Chiefly, it spares individuals the brutal effects – prison, stigma, unemployment, existence without treatment or medical care – that are legacies of the unending war. But decriminalisation alone is not enough.

It counts as a start, nevertheless, and that is more than Britain has managed. Last October, the Home Office caused strife within the coalition by publishing a report, *Drugs: International Comparators*, that looked at the experience of Portugal and a dozen other countries. To the dismay of Tories, the survey said there was "no apparent correlation" between tough laws and the level of drug use. While decriminalisation would not curb use, there were "indications that decriminalisation can reduce the burden on criminal justice systems".

Who'd have thought? In the ensuing battle, the LibDem Norman Lamb resigned as a Home Office minister while policy – "this government has absolutely no intention of decriminalising drugs" – was reaffirmed. Faced with a problem, Britain had not got beyond failing to put two and two together.

Why decriminalise? For an Irish recreational user, far less an addict, the question is superfluous. Nevertheless, O'Riordain, like his peers around the world, has taken a first step and refused the second. As the Home Office report suggested, decriminalisation has little effect on use. People go on buying their blood-stained substances and enriching some of the nastiest people on the planet. A few more police go to work hunting traffickers. Users are no longer persecuted. The mafias remain.

In 2006, the Italian journalist Roberto Saviano published *Gomorrah*, an expose, in the proper sense, of the Neapolitan Camorra. He has been forced to live since under armed guard in secret locations. Nevertheless, this summer he published *Zero Zero Zero*, a title derived from a traffickers' joke name for pure cocaine. The book is horrifying, but not just for the routine, fantastical violence. In Saviano's account, the cartels' trade has corrupted the world.

UNODC will mention "vast sums" that "compromise" economies, buy politicians and rig elections. Saviano will tell you that drugs money courses through the world's financial systems, that it touches all of us, and that it alone kept banking afloat in parts of the Americas during the great crash. He calls it narco-capitalism.

The journalist has dedicated his life to opposing the mafias. Nevertheless, in the last pages of *Zero Zero Zero* he writes: "As terrible as it may seem, total legalisation may be the only answer. A horrendous response, horrible perhaps, agonising. But the only one that can stop everything."

That strikes me as true. By one calculation, the United States alone had spent $150 billion on the drugs war by 2010. Any victories? Or just the news that Barack Obama has been commuting sentences on dozens of hapless souls locked away for life because of recreational use?

According to the Federal Bureau of Prisons, as of 26 September, 48.4 per cent of the entire US inmate population, 93,821 individuals, had been locked up for drug offences. Some war; some victory.

So legalise the lot. Those who want to use drugs will go on using drugs. In a country with common sense, like Ireland, they might get the help they need. But Saviano is right. Only one thing will put the traffickers out of business and end this hopeless war.

8 November 2015

⇨ The above information is reprinted with kind permission from *Herald Scotland*. Please visit www. heraldscotland.com for further information.

Legal highs: which drugs will be banned in the UK?

The sale of laughing gas is to be outlawed in the latest government crackdown on legal highs. Which other drugs will be affected by the ban?

By Jessica Elgot

Whether it's a high that's been around since the 17th century, or a chemical cocktail created last weekend, successive governments have found it difficult to get a grip on legal highs.

Ban one thing then tweak the compound slightly and the revamped drug becomes legal again. This is because the Misuse of Drugs Act 1971 classifies drugs as illegal by their chemical compounds.

Two new legal highs are identified in Europe every week, the European Monitoring Centre for Drugs and Drug Addiction says.

Ministers will publish a draft law on Friday to ban psychoactive substances, which would technically cover everything from coffee and cigarettes to cider, though caffeine, alcohol and nicotine are exempt, as are food and medicinal products.

The scale of the ban means that drugs used in Britain for centuries, such as laughing gas, would become illegal, as well as any new mix mimicking the effects of illegal drugs.

These are some of the drugs 'head shops' will no longer stock:

Laughing gas

Once the preserve of 15-year-olds watching Wheatus at the Reading festival, nitrous oxide has enjoyed a renaissance in recent years – despite the risk that it can cause unconsciousness from oxygen depravation.

The *Daily Mail* even published an article claiming the use of "hippy crack" had become so widespread, middle-class women were dragging on balloons in their living rooms.

Poppers

Poppers are a group of chemicals called alkyl nitrates which have become so mainstream that those shiny little bottles continue to be sold at late-night petrol stations.

As well as giving you what the national drug education service, FRANK, diplomatically terms "enhanced sexual experiences", huffing poppers gives users a sudden massive head rush. They can also cause your blood pressure to plummet to a dangerous level and can kill if swallowed.

Salvia

Salvia, a plant closely related to sage and mint, is sold as 'herbal ecstasy' and can be chewed, rolled up and smoked or inhaled through a bong.

Once the preserve of shamans in the Mazatec region of southern Mexico, its popularity has surged recently after footage of people taking it swept YouTube.

Like any hallucinogen, there's believed to be a risk salvia can trigger psychotic episodes. Or you could just end up looking as daft as the people on YouTube.

Spice (synthetic cannabinoids)

Remember how horror stories of meow meow, m-kat and benzo fury made headlines after a spate of deaths, and was quickly banned? Spice was poised to be the next dangerous drug at the centre of such a controversy after it was linked to several deaths.

Many of the chemicals in cannabinoids, which can be ordered online and have a variety of stupid names such as clockwork orange, black mamba, annihilation and devil's weed, are illegal under the Misuse of Drugs Act. But because police can't be sure of the exact cocktail of chemicals in the packets, the Government thought it best to ban everything.

Alcohol substitutes

Prof. David Nutt, the drugs adviser fired by the Government for his views on ecstasy, is part of a team developing 'alcosynth', billed as a safer alternative to alcohol.

Nutt says the pill mimics the tipsy sensation felt after a few lagers, without the street brawling and liver damage. But although alcohol is exempt under new regulation, the synthetic alcohol is not, so Nutt's new drug will be banned.

29 May 2015

⇨ The above information is reprinted with kind permission from *The Guardian*. Please visit www.theguardian.com for further information.

Legal highs: regulation won't work – the only answer lies in prevention

An article from The Conversation.   THE C⊙NVERSATION

By Fabrizio Schifano, Chair in Clinical Pharmacology and Therapeutics, University of Hertfordshire

In one respect, the world's drug problem is not getting much worse. The UN believes that the use of drugs such as cocaine and heroin has stabilised, for example. In fact, the ground in the drugs battle has just shifted. The focus is now increasingly on legal highs.

People might be aware that altered versions of ecstasy or cannabis are available nowadays, but the true range of what we in the trade call novel psychoactive drugs is far more varied. There are derivatives of everything from ketamine to cocaine, from opiates to psychotropics. Their use is rising, and so is the number of fatalities. Some people fear that the figures are only going in one direction.

Enforcers vs chemists

Why has this happened? In recent years there was a worldwide decrease in the purity of drugs like amphetamine and cocaine and the MDMA content of ecstasy. This decrease helped fuel demand for alternatives (though admittedly there are signs that this purity decrease is now reversing). The internet has also made possible the sort of sharing of information that makes it much easier to sell these substances nowadays. And as has been well documented, banning these drugs is difficult because the manufacturers can constantly bring out new varieties with slight alterations to the chemistry.

It has turned into a battle between the drug enforcers and the drug chemists, who are typically based in the Far East, for example in China and Hong Kong. There are many databases online with information on the molecular structures of existing drugs. This makes it easier for these people to modify them to create a new product.

The market is very strong in the UK. You might think it is because the information online is often written in English. This would explain why Ireland has a big problem too, but then again the US does not. And other problem countries include Latvia, Hungary, Estonia and Russia.

The big worries

Certain categories particularly worry us. One is the ecstasy derivatives known as phenethylamines. One of the well-known ones in the UK is PMA, which has been nicknamed 'Dr Death' because of the number of fatalities. Another is known as 'blue mystique'. These have been made illegal in a number of European countries, but many more keep appearing. A related group is known as NBOMe, which are very powerful and therefore also a great concern.

Then there are cannabimimetics, which are sometimes known as the 'spice drugs'. There are a few hundred known variations, many of which are very powerful, sometimes thousands of times more than cannabis. They were behind the 'spiceophrenia' epidemic in Russia, but are prevalent closer to home too. Last week a new HM Prisons report mentioned them among a number of legal-high concerns in British prisons. To make matters worse, they are very easy to modify and have the big selling point that they can't always be traced in urine.

Sometimes legal highs are marketed as a solution to a problem that an illegal drug might cause. For example ketamine ('special K') is known to damage the intestine and bladder, so a new drug reached the market called methoxetamine, or 'special M,' which claimed to be bladder-friendly. But in fact it is still toxic for the bladder and also the kidney and central nervous system. And after it was made illegal, a number of other derivatives appeared such as diphenidine. The health risks associated with this class makes the new versions particularly scary.

The unwinnable battle?

We often don't know how these drugs affect people. Researchers like myself are working on this, but the number of new substances is increasing too quickly for us to keep up. By the time we publish papers focusing on more popular versions, the market has changed. When something goes wrong, doctors don't know how to treat the effects – in many cases they can't even ascertain the exact drug.

We have reached the point where I am now more worried about legal highs than illegal drugs. Whenever I see a heroin client in my clinic, I know exactly what to do. That is often not the case with legal highs. And as a psychiatrist I know that they potentially have far more psychiatric consequences than heroin. Whenever you tamper with very sensitive mechanisms in your brain, it's difficult to know what will happen.

One argument is that we should keep these drugs legal since we

are facing an unwinnable battle. But the big drawback with this is that it makes adolescents and other susceptible people think that the drug must be safe. New Zealand tried this approach by permitting drugs to remain in circulation if the producers could demonstrate they were low risk, but this year the Government U-turned after there were a number of adverse incidents. Now its approach is similar to the UK with its expanding prohibition schedule.

The problem with the New Zealand low-risk policy is that establishing the safety of a drug is a very slow process if you are going to do it properly. Proving through clinical trials that a drug works, is safe and is not toxic takes upwards of ten years. Anything less would be cutting corners. If a manufacturer were to go through that process and prove that a drug was low risk, that might be a different

discussion, but it's not going to help with today's problem.

Similarly there has been some debate about permitting the supply of legal highs but keeping it tightly restricted – perhaps allowing one distributor per town, for example. But this both ignores the reality of the Internet and offers no answer to the safety problem.

Another possibility is to legalise the illegal drugs that we know much more about, so that people are encouraged to take them instead. But even if this was politically possible, it doesn't sound like the right course of action either. I see disasters from drug-taking on a daily basis. And it wouldn't necessarily stop people from taking legal highs anyway.

The answer to what we actually should do is complex. The answer probably lies in prevention: we need dedicated resources and funding, we need new ideas to try and convince youngsters that these drugs are not safe just because they are legal. This requires a big change in how we see these substances. These are not just some marginal concern. This is the new drug battle for the decades ahead.

29 October 2014

⇨ The above information is reprinted with kind permission from *The Conversation*. Please visit www.theconversation.com for further information.

Men are more likely to take drugs than women

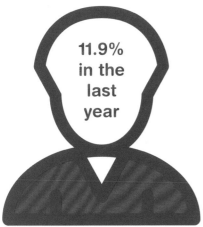

11.9% in the last year

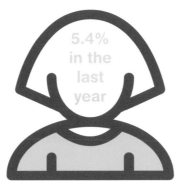

5.4% in the last year

Source: Drug misuse, findings from the 2014/15 Crime Survey for England and Wales, *Home Office*

What does it mean to have an addiction?

An addiction is when a person has lost control over doing, taking or using something. It's possible to become addicted to anything, but some addictions are more damaging than others.

What are addictions?

A person who is addicted to something can't control how they use it, or need it to get through everyday life.

Addictions can be to substances, like alcohol, tobacco or other drugs, or to behaviours, like gambling or extreme exercise.

Addictions are a problem when they start to affect health in a bad way or interfere with a person's ability to lead a normal life, as well as the people around them.

Why do addictions happen?

A person might start to take a drug or engage in an activity because it's enjoyable and not have a problem with it at first.

They might do it because they feel it helps them relax or to cope with stress by covering up bad feelings.

As time goes by, the person might find they need to do or take more of a thing to get the same effect. They can soon feel they need to take or do the thing to feel 'normal'.

What are physical addictions?

Some substances make changes to our bodies so that, over time, our bodies really do 'need' the substance to work normally. If they don't get enough of it, the person gets cravings or 'withdrawal'.

However, even if they do get the substance they are addicted to, it may still be damaging their health in other ways. Addiction often

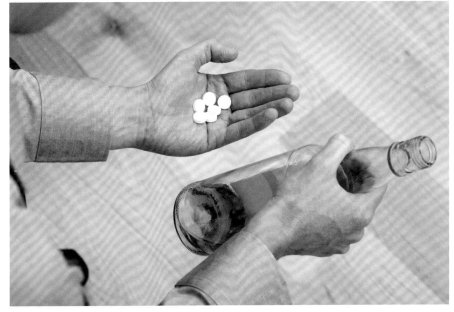

damages other areas of their lives like money, their relationships, studies and career.

Are you living with someone with an addiction?

Living with or just being around people who have problems with alcohol, drugs or other addictions can be hard.

It can be especially hard on you if you have to cope with this alone.

It's important that you talk to someone about what's happening and get support where you can.

If you can't speak to a trusted friend, teacher or relative, call ChildLine free at any time on 0800 1111.

Help for addictions

Help, support and advice is available for people with addictions to help them get better.

Lots of people turn to their doctor first, and this can be a good place to start.

Support groups can help people work through the problems around their substance abuse or behaviour.

Psychiatrists, psychologists, nurses and doctors can also help, and there are lots of helplines and websites to turn to.

⇨ The above information is reprinted with kind permission from Young Scot. Please visit young.scot for further information.

© Young Scot 2016

What is dependence?

When you take drugs like heroin (opioids) on a regular basis, changes take place in your brain and nervous system so you need to continue taking the drug just to feel normal.

"Everyone's level of dependence is different, and it can be difficult to realise when you've crossed the line from use to dependence"

What's more, your body keeps on changing, adapting its own responses so that often more and more drugs are needed just to get through the day. With drug dependence's acute (or short-term) symptoms – like cravings and withdrawal – and its chronic (or long-term) effects – like depression and liver damage – it's little wonder that a lot of users say that they feel "out of control" and that drugs have taken over their lives. For many, treatment offers a way to get some control back over their brain, their body and their life.

Stigma and exclusion

Using heroin and similar drugs has been heavily stigmatised in the past – just like having a disability or a mental health problem has been. But times are changing: a 2009 public opinion poll for the charity DrugScope found that 19% of people had a direct or close experience of a drug problem. That's one in five people who have some understanding of what you are going through. The same opinion poll found a massive 88% of people support the state providing drug treatment for people who want to address their problems.

Of course this doesn't mean that everyone will be understanding of your situation, or that your recovery journey won't have moments when you feel people are judging you, but it does mean that things are getting better.

Remember that you are not alone, there are support groups out there that can help. Recovery from dependence is possible and people have been through similar experiences to you. A selection of personal 'Stories of survival' videos are available for you to watch on our website, we hope you find them encouraging and useful.

Most people now recognise that people with drug dependency have a medical problem and need treatment. And like any other medical condition treatment is really important. In the short term, stabilising your symptoms should be the first priority: reducing the harm you do to yourself and others, minimising withdrawal, reducing cravings and the frequency of use. In the long term, getting away from a lifestyle that is centred around your opioid dependence and tackling some of the reasons why you used drugs in the first place may help you move towards recovery.

My Recovery My Choice can help you find out more about the ways that you can move forward from here and how to begin the journey. If you have tried, unsuccessfully, to stop using heroin in the past then you are not alone. The majority of people try and fail at least once. If you are no stranger to treatment, it may be worth taking the time to read through your recovery options to find out what's new, both in terms of your choices and what is known about them. If you are worried about a friend or family member who might have a problem, the information here can help you start a conversation with them, and help them start their journey.

Is it a problem?

Dependence on heroin and other opioids doesn't happen overnight but usually develops over a period of continued substance use. Everyone's level of dependence is different, and it can be difficult to realise when you've crossed the line from use to dependence.

Have a look at the list below. These are the kind of things which might be going on in your life when your drug use shifts into dependency. The more you can identify with the things on this list, the more likely it is that you're dependent.

⇨ "It's not just weekends"... I'm using heroin for longer periods.

⇨ "I need a lot more"... the same dose of heroin doesn't give me the same feeling as it used to.

⇨ "I can't seem to stop"... I've tried to stop using heroin but despite my efforts I have not been able to.

⇨ "They've said it's a problem"... I've been asked by my partner or family to stop using heroin.

⇨ "I'm rattling"... I experience withdrawal symptoms (aches and pains, sweats, restlessness) when I stop using heroin.

⇨ "I can't stop thinking about it"... I've got heroin – how I'm going to get it, when I'm going to get it – going around my mind all the time.

⇨ "I don't want to but"... I've continued to use heroin/opioids despite negative consequences.

⇨ "It's 24/7"... I spend lots of time and effort, even committing crime, to obtain or use heroin.

⇨ "It's my main thing now"... I've missed work, stopped seeing non-drug-using mates or started going out just so that I can use heroin.

⇨ The above information is reprinted with kind permission from My Recovery My Choice. Please visit www.myrecoverymychoice.co.uk for further information.

© My Recovery My Choice 2016

Drug addiction: getting help

If you have a problem with drugs, there's a wide range of addiction services that can help.

Some of these services are provided by the NHS, and some are specialist drug facilities run by charities and private organisations.

You can use the search to locate your nearest NHS drug addiction support services.

This guide to getting treatment for a drug problem will steer you through the options, so you can find help that works for you. If you have a problem with drugs, you have the same entitlement to care as anyone coming to the NHS for help with any other health problem.

With the right help and support it's possible for you to get drug free and stay that way.

Where to get help for drugs

A good place to start is to visit your GP. Your GP can discuss your concerns with you, assess the nature of your problems and help you choose the most appropriate treatment. Your GP might offer to treat you or might refer you to your local specialist drug service.

Many drug treatment services accept self-referrals so, if you're not comfortable talking to your GP, you might be able to approach your local drug treatment service directly.

You can find information about local drug treatment services on the FRANK website.

If you're having trouble finding the right sort of help, call the FRANK drugs helpline on 0300 123 6600. An adviser can talk to you about the different options.

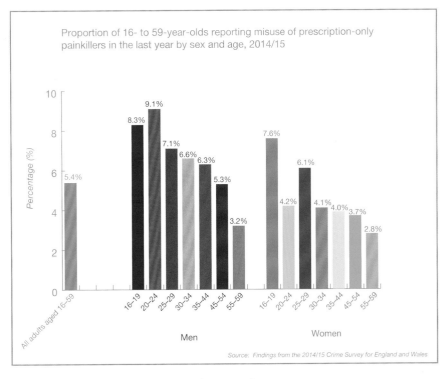

Proportion of 16- to 59-year-olds reporting misuse of prescription-only painkillers in the last year by sex and age, 2014/15

Source: Findings from the 2014/15 Crime Survey for England and Wales

Your drugs keyworker

If you are seen at your local drug treatment service, you will first be assessed and, if you are deemed appropriate for treatment, you will then be allocated a keyworker. Your keyworker may be a doctor, a nurse or a drugs worker.

Your keyworker will help you organise the treatment that you need, develop a personalised care plan with you and be your first point of call throughout your treatment. You'll see your keyworker for regular one-to-one sessions during your treatment.

Charity and private drugs treatment

Outside the NHS, there are many voluntary sector and private drug and alcohol treatment organisations that can help you. As well as residential rehab centres, community services of various types are provided by voluntary organisations. These include structured day programmes, outreach and harm reduction services, counselling services, aftercare and housing support services.

These organisations will usually be linked to NHS services in your area.

8 October 2014

⇨ The above information is reprinted with kind permission from NHS Choices. Please visit www.nhs.uk for further information.

Therapy for children of drug users to be researched for NHS by Scottish university

A therapy could be used to improve the health and happiness of children in the UK is being researched by Scottish academics in a £230,000 research programme.

Academics from Edinburgh Napier University will work with Harvard Medical School to assess whether Behavioural Couples Therapy (BCT) could be used in the NHS.

Edinburgh Napier's Dr Anne Whittaker and Professor Lawrie Elliott will work with Harvard Medical School's Professor Timothy O'Farrell.

The 22-month feasibility study – the first to examine the potential for BCT in the UK – will explore the impact of the therapy on 18 Scots families in which one or both parents is being treated for drug misuse.

Evidence shows that the children of drug users are often ill-treated and that they are more likely to develop substance misuse problems themselves.

Research shows that BCT has been effective in reducing emotional problems among young people with a parent with drug use issues.

The feasibility study will see BCT – which involves working with couples to improve communication and relationships, and reduce drug use – being delivered at NHS Lothian's Substance Misuse Directorate.

Research staff will ask parents and clinical staff taking part in the programme to gather information on the benefits and drawbacks before a decision is taken on whether to proceed with a pilot trial.

Dr Whittaker, who was seconded from NHS Lothian to Edinburgh Napier with a remit to develop research into addictions, said: "NHS addiction services desperately need to find more effective ways of helping children and families affected by parental drug use.

"Our review of the evidence found that BCT could make a real difference to parents who are struggling with an addiction and the beauty of this intervention is that it does not directly involve the children but, nevertheless, can improve their lives significantly.

"The intervention needs to be delivered by skilled professionals which is why we are testing this within the NHS where qualified mental health nurses and clinical psychologists can deliver BCT to the standard required."

24 August 2015

⇨ The above information is reprinted with kind permission from *Herald Scotland*. Please visit www.heraldscotland.com for further information.

Why addiction affects some people but not others

Many people around the UK drink alcohol moderately and never become addicted to it. The same can be said of some individuals who have experimented with illegal drugs. However, there are thousands of people in Britain struggling every day with addiction to these substances. So why do some people become addicted while others do not?

The reality is that anyone can become addicted. Addiction is not something that happens to just one type of person. It affects men, women, young, old and those from all cultures, religious persuasion, political leanings, sexual orientation, etc. It does not discriminate. Nevertheless, there are a number of factors that are said to increase the risk of developing an addiction. Here are a few examples:

Genetics

It has recently been suggested that family genes can make some individuals more disposed to addiction. But that does not necessarily mean that because a person has a parent who suffered from addiction that he or she will too. It is generally accepted that there is more than one gene involved that can make a person susceptible to addiction. In some cases, an individual may have the genes but these are never activated.

According to scientists, genes are responsible for 50 per cent of the risk of developing alcoholism and 75 per cent of the risk of developing a drug addiction. And evidence suggests that children of parents with alcoholism are four times more likely to become alcoholics themselves.

Age

The earlier a person experiments with drugs or alcohol then the more likely they are to develop an addiction. Many people who have suffered from addiction started using drugs or drinking alcohol before the age of 21. Young people who dabble with drugs and alcohol in their early teens have a much higher chance of developing an addiction than those who do not.

Environment

Where a person grows up can play a role in their risk of developing an addiction. For example, if drug addiction and alcoholism are commonplace in the area in which a person lives, this individual is more likely to try drugs and alcohol and, therefore, more liable to become addicted than a person who has never had any exposure to these substances. Other factors such as relationships with family and friends, quality of life, stress, economic status and peer pressure can all increase the risk as well.

Mental health problems

Studies have shown that those with mental health problems – such as anxiety, stress, depression, bipolar disorder and post-traumatic stress disorder – have a much greater risk of becoming addicted to substances such as drugs or alcohol.

Trauma

Traumatic events can increase a person's risk of developing an addiction. Those who have experienced trauma in their lives may turn to drugs or alcohol to numb the pain. Events such as bereavement, domestic violence, emotional, physical or sexual abuse, or living with an addicted parent can all increase the risk. People who have had more than one traumatic event in their lives are even more likely to be affected by addiction.

Although the above are factors that increase a person's risk of developing an addiction, they do not necessarily mean it will happen. Many individuals have all of the above but do not go on to use drugs or drink alcohol.

What to do if you have a problem

If you are worried about the amount of alcohol you are drinking, or find that you are taking too many illegal or prescription drugs, contact Addiction Helper today. Our team of expert advisors can give you the information required about the current treatments available. We can help you overcome your problems and will put you in touch with a suitable provider based on your circumstances. Call us today for advice and support.

22 October 2015

⇨ The above information is reprinted with kind permission from Addiction Helper. www. addictionhelper.com.

Is getting teenage kicks today a direct line to drug addiction?

By Kelvin Graham

Parents catching sight of recent press headlines might be anxiously wondering if their own teenage son or daughter's constant lack of a good night's sleep is more than just about kids being on social media sites 24/7.

Four in ten teenagers...

New research has found that nearly four in ten teenagers in the UK said they had taken substances, including cannabis and ecstasy, according to the European School Survey Project on Alcohol and Other Drugs (ESPAD).

The survey questioned 15- and 16-year-olds from schools in 30 European countries. Of the 223 schools in the UK which participated, 36 per cent of teenagers admitted to trying an illegal drug. There are 5.4 million teenagers in the UK (Office of National Statistics), so that could mean some 1.9 million youngsters are at potential risk of substance abuse and addiction.

Too far-fetched, you say? In 2014, figures released by the Home Office showed that illicit drug use in England and Wales rose by an estimated 230,000 to 2.7 million over the previous year. Nearly 80 per cent or 180,000 of the extra users were teenagers and young adults aged 16 to 24, who made up 1.1 million of the total number.

It may not be too alarmist to point to further evidence of drug use appearing to be growing among Britain's youngsters...

Drugs used include cannabis, crack cocaine...

More than 2,000 incidents over the last four years involve school children, one as young as eight years old, according to figures recently obtained from around 30 police forces under the Freedom of Information Act. The drugs used include cannabis, crack cocaine, LSD and ecstasy.

While nearly 80 per cent of youngsters aged between 11 and 15 say they have never taken drugs, according to children's drug protection charity, Mentor UK, the organisation also says an estimated 360,000 secondary school-aged pupils in England took at least one drug in the previous year.

The one drug is likely to be cannabis – the most widely used illegal drug, according to Mentor UK with 7.5 per cent of secondary school pupils and 14 per cent of 16- to 19-year-olds saying they took the drug in the last year.

"Don't Panic..."

It's obviously worrying news. Some parents who might have dabbled with a few recreational 'soft' drugs in their younger days are sure to be aware that over the decades the strength of many – most famously, "skunk" cannabis – have been increased many times over to dangerously high levels.

So what to do if you're worried your teenage son or daughter may be taking drugs?

Firstly, "Don't Panic", as Corporal Jones from *Dad's Army* would say! It's important to start talking things over with your growing young adult, find out a little bit more about their world, their friends and any peer pressure they may feel under to become involved with taking drugs.

No doubt you will be told in no uncertain terms that they "can handle it, no problem" but ultimately, you may need to seek professional advice if you suspect there is a problem. The key is not to get angry but always to listen before passing them the benefit of your experience on the left hand side...

April 2015

⇨ The above information is reprinted with kind permission from Help 4 Addiction. Please visit www. help4addiction.co.uk for further information.

They think I have a drugs/alcohol problem

When friends or family members get on your case about taking drugs or drinking alcohol it might seem unfair, but there are ways of handling the situation so that you are both happy.

You started with a bit of weed, but now you're smoking every day and you can't be bothered getting up for work or college any more. Maybe you're partial to the odd beer or ten, and your hangovers leave you begging for a dark room and a couple of cans to get you back on your feet. Or do you knock back a few ecstasy pills at the weekend then feel like the comedown is lasting all week?

So now your parents have started noticing what a stinking mood you're in and they're giving you grief about it. Or your sister is giving you a hard time after she found king-size papers in your room. Maybe your partner is nagging that things have got to change otherwise they're leaving you? And you're left wondering why they don't just get off your case and leave you alone.

I don't think I have a drugs/ alcohol problem!

If your drug or alcohol use has reached a point where other people have noticed or are getting involved – by nagging you to stop, begging you to change or even completely disowning you, the chances are they are viewing it as a problem. You might not see it as an issue, but if you do, it's annoying that they're all butting into your life.

Jenny is now 24 but was using large amounts of ecstasy, speed and cocaine between the ages of 15 to 18. At the time, she wasn't that concerned about the effect it was having on her family and friends, but her situation escalated to the point where her she completely alienated the people who cared about her.

"My friends hated the way I changed into a moody cow who only cared about going out at the weekends," she says. "My best mate at school said I had to choose between her and drugs. At the time I just laughed at her and said there was no competition. We didn't speak for years after that."

How are you making others feel?

Looking back on her situation, Jenny can see how wrapped up she was in drugs and how she didn't really consider anyone else around her. "I think users only see what they want to see and don't realise the hurt they can cause," says Jenny. "They can become very self-centred and anyone who doesn't share their love of drugs is seen as ignorant."

Though you may find it difficult to consider the feelings of your parents, siblings, friends or partner, doing so can help you communicate with them better, which will only improve your situation in the long term.

Louise, a parent and family worker in a substance misuse service, has a brother who is heroin dependent. "When we found out about my brother my family was in shock. We knew nothing about drugs and were frightened about what could happen to him," she says.

This is a normal response; you may be on familiar territory, but your family is often in the dark when it comes to what your lifestyle actually involves. Think about it – while it might just seem like a few bongs or a couple of lines of coke to you, to your dad, who has a limited experience of drug taking, you could already be on the road to ruin.

"If your family or friends have actually started asking you questions about drugs, one of the best things you can do is talk to them," says Louise. "Their imagination about what's happening is usually a hundred times worse than the reality. Once your drug use is out in the open, lying and keeping secrets only increases anxiety and makes relationships suffer."

How to get on with each other

Whether or not you're feeling ready to change your behaviour, or whether you even want to, it will be a long while before people will realise that they can't make you change. Finding ways to keep them on your side will help enormously in easing tensions on the home front. It could also stop you from losing the people who care about you, as Jenny did.

Be proactive and responsible to show them that at least you will look after yourself. Go to a drug advice centre and find out all the information you need about the substances you're using (even if it's booze – you may be surprised at how little you know). You can also make a harm reduction plan along with the people who are concerned about you. For example, always tell them where you are going, tell a friend what drugs you are taking, and don't mix with other drugs or alcohol.

Feeling fearful is a major reason why family members try to force you into help you might not want. Point them in the direction of a family drug worker who will support them and help to improve communication between everyone.

Jenny adds: "Remember that their concerns stem from love and worry, they only want you to be OK. I just thought my mates were jealous of what a great time I was having, I didn't realise how much I was scaring them."

The above information is reprinted with kind permission from The Mix – Essential support for under 25s (www. themixuk.org)

TheMixUK.org is the guide to life for under 25-year-olds in the UK. We provide non-judgmental support and information on everything from sex and exam stress to debt and drugs.

*Our straight-talking emotional support is available 24 hours a day. On TheMixUK.org you can: * Chat about anything you like on our moderated discussion boards and live chat room.*

* Browse over 2,000 articles and videos full of facts you can trust.

* Read about the experiences of other young people in our True Life section.

* Call us free on 0808 808 4994 (every day 11am-11pm).

Treatment for drug addiction could be used to tackle sugar addiction, experts say

"It may represent a novel new treatment strategy to tackle the obesity epidemic."

By Natasha Hinde

People with sugar addiction could be treated with the same methods used to treat those with drug addiction, research has suggested.

Researchers from Queensland University of Technology conducted a study which found drugs used to treat nicotine addiction could also be used to treat sugar addiction – and therefore tackle the obesity epidemic.

There are currently 1.9 billion people worldwide who are overweight, with 600 million considered obese, according to the World Health Organization.

Excess sugar consumption has been proven to contribute directly to weight gain. It also elevates dopamine levels, which control the brain's reward and pleasure centres.

Researchers likened the effect sugar has on the brain to drugs such as tobacco, cocaine and morphine.

"After long-term consumption, this leads to the opposite, a reduction in dopamine levels," explained Professor Selena Bartlett from QUT's Institute of Health and Biomedical Innovation.

"This leads to higher consumption of sugar to get the same level of reward."

"We have also found that as well as an increased risk of weight gain, animals that maintain high sugar consumption and binge-eating into adulthood may also face neurological and psychiatric consequences affecting mood and motivation."

According to researchers, drugs like varenicline, a prescription medication which treats nicotine addiction, can work the same way when it comes to sugar cravings.

PhD researcher Masroor Shariff said the study also put artificial sweeteners under the spotlight.

"Interestingly, our study also found that artificial sweeteners such as saccharin could produce effects similar to those we obtained with table sugar, highlighting the importance of reevaluating our relationship with sweetened food per se," he said.

Professor Bartlett said varenicline acted as a "neuronal nicotinic receptor modulator" and similar results were observed with other such drugs including mecamylamine and cytisine.

"Like other drugs of abuse, withdrawal from chronic sucrose exposure can result in an imbalance in dopamine levels and be as difficult as going 'cold turkey' from them," she said.

"Further studies are required but our results do suggest that current FDA-approved nAChR drugs may represent a novel new treatment strategy to tackle the obesity epidemic."

The study has been published in the journal *PLOS ONE.*

13 April 2016

⇨ The above information is reprinted with kind permission from The Huffington Post UK. Please visit www.huffingtonpost.co.uk for further information.

Key facts

⇨ According to a recent survey, only 2% of pupils who said their parents did not like them to drink had drunk alcohol in the last week, compared to 44% of those whose parents did not mind. (page 4)

⇨ Around one in 12 (8.6%) adults aged 16 to 59 have taken an illicit drug in the last year. This equates to around 2.8 million people. (page 5)

⇨ People living in urban areas reported higher levels of drug use than those living in rural areas. Just under a tenth (9.1%) of people living in urban areas had used any drug compared with 6.5% of those living in rural areas. In addition, higher levels of drug use are associated with increased frequency of visits to pubs, bars and nightclubs. (page 5)

⇨ Use of New Psychoactive Substances (NPS) in the last year appears to be concentrated among young adults aged 16 to 24. Around one in 40 (2.8%) young adults aged 16 to 24 took an NPS in the last year, while fewer than one in 100 (0.9%) of 16- to 59-year-olds had done so. This equates to around 174,000 young adults aged 16 to 24 and 279,000 adults 16 to 59. (page 5)

⇨ The use of ecstasy in the last year increased among 16- to 24-year-olds between the 2013/14 and 2014/15 surveys, from 3.9% to 5.4%. This is an increase of approximately 95,000 young people. (page 5)

⇨ Mephedrone (68%), ecstasy (57%), amphetamines (50%) and tranquillisers (35%) are the drugs most likely to be used simultaneously with other drugs. (page 5)

⇨ In a recent survey, TV was consistently the most mentioned media source of helpful information about drugs over the last five years. In 2013, 59% of pupils mentioned TV as a source of helpful information about drugs, ahead of the Internet (53%). However, the impact of the government-funded website FRANK has fallen in recent years, from 36% in 2009 to 18% in 2013. (page 13)

⇨ A survey published in 2014, which was carried out by NatCen Social Research finds that 69% of 11- to 15-year-olds say that teachers are a helpful source of information about taking drugs, up from 63% in 2009. Almost as many pupils (68%) said their parents were also helpful sources. (page 13)

⇨ Almost two million people across England and Wales are abusing prescription painkillers either to get high or relax, according to a survey. (page 13)

⇨ Last year in the Greater Glasgow area, 3,339 individuals who injected SIEDs attended a needle exchange, in contrast to 7,670 who inject heroin. (page 16)

⇨ Over 100 new and unpredictable synthetic substances were recorded in 2014 by the European Monitoring Centre for Drugs and Drug Addiction (EMCDDA). As a result, the number of deaths linked to the use of legal highs has escalated eightfold in three years, according to the Centre for Social Justice (CSJ). (page 17)

⇨ The number of police incidents involving 'legal highs' has almost trebled across England in a year, new figures obtained by the Centre for Social Justice (CSJ) reveal. Incidents soared across forces – from 1,356 in 2013 to 3,652 in 2014 (an increase of 169 per cent). But the overall number will be much higher as 12 of England's 39 police forces did not respond to the freedom of information request, including the Metropolitan Police. (page 18)

⇨ Levels of HIV, closely associated with needle injection around the world, are very low among British injectors, largely thanks to the harm-reduction policies pioneered by Norman Fowler when he was Margaret Thatcher's Health secretary in the 1980s. In the USA, up to 20% of injectors have HIV; in Byisk, in Russia, it's more than 70%. But in England, the rate is just over 2%. (page 23)

⇨ In 2000, Portugal decriminalised the use of all illicit drugs, and developed new policies on prevention, treatment, harm reduction and reinsertion. (page 28)

⇨ In China, drug possession for personal use is technically classified as a minor administrative offence but punishment can be harsh – a 2,000 RMB fine and up to 15 days of administrative detention. (page 29)

⇨ 11.9% of men used drugs in the last year, compared to 5.4% of women. (page 32)

⇨ In 2014, figures released by the Home Office showed that illicit drug use in England and Wales rose by an estimated 230,000 to 2.7 million over the previous year. Nearly 80 per cent or 180,000 of the extra users were teenagers and young adults aged 16 to 24, who made up 1.1 million of the total number. (page 37)

Addiction

A dependence on a substance which makes it very difficult to stop taking it. Addiction can be either physical, meaning the user's body has become dependent on the substance and will suffer negative symptoms if the substance is withdrawn, or psychological, meaning a user has no physical need to take a substance, but will experience strong cravings if it is withdrawn.

Amphetamines

Synthetic drugs which can be swallowed, inhaled or injected. Their effects can include increased mental alertness, energy and confidence. Most amphetamines are Class B substances, but crystal meth and prepared-for-injection speed are Class A. Taking amphetamines can cause anxiety or paranoia and risks include overdose and psychological dependence. They can also put strain on a user's heart, leading to cardiac problems.

Depressant

A substance that slows down the nervous system, making the user feel calmer and more relaxed. These drugs are also known as 'downers' and include alcohol, heroin and tranquillisers.

Detox

Ridding the body of toxins, i.e. drugs.

Drug

A chemical that alters the way the mind and body works. Legal drugs include alcohol, tobacco, caffeine and prescription medicines taken for medical reasons. Illegal drugs taken for recreation include cannabis, cocaine, ecstasy and speed. These illegal substances are divided into three classes – A, B and C – according to the danger they pose to the user and to society (with A being the most harmful and C the least).

Drug driving law

In the UK it is illegal to drive if you are unfit to do so because you are taking legal or illegal drugs, or if you have certain levels of illegal drugs in your blood.

Hallucinogen

A drug which produces visions and sensations detached from reality (a 'trip'). Common hallucinogens include LSD, ketamine and magic mushrooms.

Legal high

Also known as psychoactive substances, legal highs function as stimulants and have mood altering properties. Producing or trading in these substances will become illegal in the UK in 2016.

Misuse of Drugs Act 1971

Legislation prohibiting the use of dangerous recreational substances, making it an offence to possess banned drugs for personal use or with the intent to supply. It also divides drugs into three classes according to the degree of harm they pose to the individual and to society – A, B or C – each with different associated penalties.

Needle exchange

A service that allows drug users to obtain safe, clean, hypodermic needles.

Opiate

A drug that is derived from opium, e.g. heroin.

Overdose

This occurs when an individual takes such a large dose of a drug that their body cannot cope with the effects. An overdose can cause organ failure, coma and death.

Psychoactive Substances Act

The Psychoactive Substances Act makes it a criminal offence to produce or supply any psychoactive substance. The Act is designed to stop people from trading in 'legal highs'. Possessing a psychoactive substance will not be an offence.

Reclassification

When an illegal substance is moved from one drugs class into another, after its harmfulness has been reassessed or new research has uncovered previously-unknown negative effects.

Stimulant

A volatile substance which gives off fumes. Vapours from products including paint, glue and aerosols can be inhaled and cause intoxication. Volatile substance abuse is highly dangerous, killing more children aged ten to 15 than all illegal drugs put together.

Withdrawal

Symptoms experienced when 'withdrawing' from substance use.

Assignments

Brainstorming

⇨ In small groups, discuss what you know about drug abuse?

- Why do people take drugs?

- Can you become addiction to non-illegal drugs, such as prescription painkillers?

- What is a 'legal high'?

Research

⇨ Using online newspaper archives, do some research about over-the-counter medicine misuse. Write a bullet point list of stories and issues you discover around this theme.

⇨ Research the recent introduction of a drug-driving law in the UK. Write a summary of the legislation and share with your classmates.

⇨ Using the table on page 20, create a graph to illustrate the proportion of 16- to 59-year-olds reporting the use of Class A drugs in their lifetime. Think carefully about the type of graph you should use, and create more than one if necessary.

⇨ Research drugs laws in a different country and write 500 words exploring whether their policy is more effective than policy in the UK.

⇨ Research treatment programmes for drug addiction. What do they involve? Discuss with a partner.

Design

⇨ Choose one of the types of drugs mentioned in the article *Get the facts about drugs* on page 1. Create a poster that illustrates the risks associated with your chosen drug.

⇨ Design a campaign that warns young people about the dangers of risky behaviour such as drug taking. Your campaign could be based in print, social media or television adverts. Work in groups of three or four and write at least 500 words to explain your campaign. Include examples such as storyboards or mock-up posters if necessary.

⇨ Design a horizontal banner that could be displayed as an advert on websites to highlight the dangers of legal highs.

⇨ Choose one of the articles from this book and create an illustration that highlights the key themes of the piece.

Oral

⇨ Imagine that you are concerned about your friend's use of cannabis. Write an e-mail to your friend explaining why you are concerned and giving advice about where they could turn for help.

⇨ The findings from the 2014/15 crime survey suggest that young people are more likely to take drugs than older people. In small groups discuss why you think this might be.

⇨ In pairs, go through this book and discuss the cartoons you come across. Think about what the artists were trying to portray with each illustration.

⇨ Create a PowerPoint presentation that explains the effect different types of drugs have on the brain.

⇨ In pairs, discuss why you think 'more young people are turning to teachers for drugs advice'.

⇨ According to the article *Detox or lose your benefits...* on page 26, a recent Government proposal suggests that if people don't accept help for drink or drugs-related problems, they will lose their benefits. As a class, discuss whether you think this is a good idea.

⇨ Create a storyboard for a TV ad campaign that will highlight the legal consequences of drug use. The campaign should be aimed at teenagers and explain the penalties for using Class A, B and C drugs. Most importantly, it should demonstrate the long-term impact that a criminal record could have on their lives.

⇨ Do you think binge drinking is a more serious problem than illegal drug use in the UK? Why is drinking more socially acceptable than drug taking? List your thoughts and then discuss with a partner.

Reading/writing

⇨ Read the article *Smoking, drinking and drug use...* on page 4 and write a summary for your school newspaper.

⇨ Watch the film *Trainspotting*. Is its portrayal of heroin addicts in 90s Edinburgh still relevant to the UK today? Think about the effect that drug abuse has on the characters' relationships, health and lifestyle. Write a review of the film.

⇨ Write a letter to your local MP explaining the importance of adapting needle and syringe exchanges to meet the needs of people who inject steroids (see page 15 for helpful information).

⇨ Imagine that you are one of a team of people organising a summer festival. Write a report for your colleagues about the dangers of illegal highs and why you are concerned about their use at the festival. You should include suggestions for steps that could be taken to limit their use.

Acknowledgements

The publisher is grateful for permission to reproduce the material in this book. While every care has been taken to trace and acknowledge copyright, the publisher tenders its apology for any accidental infringement or where copyright has proved untraceable. The publisher would be pleased to come to a suitable arrangement in any such case with the rightful owner.

Images

All images courtesy of iStock, except page 17: Pexels and page 24 © Jackie Staines.

Icons on page 32 and 41 are made by Freepik from www.flaticon.com

Illustrations

Don Hatcher: pages 2 & 12. Simon Kneebone: pages 10 & 18. Angelo Madrid: pages 16 & 25.

Additional acknowledgements

Editorial on behalf of Independence Educational Publishers by Cara Acred.

With thanks to the Independence team: Mary Chapman, Sandra Dennis, Christina Hughes, Jackie Staines and Jan Sunderland.

Cara Acred

Cambridge

May 2016